Clare

AND TIMELESS ART COLLECTION OF J. J. HAVERTY

To George,

WILLIAM RAWSON SMITH

William Rawson Smith

Best Wishes

MERCER UNIVERSITY PRESS
2006

MERCER UNIVERSITY PRESS
1400 Coleman Avenue | Macon, Georgia 31207 | www.mupress.org
MUP / H711 | FIRST EDITION

Printed in the United States of America

Library of Congress Cataloging-in-Publication Data

Smith, William Rawson. Villa Clare: the purposeful life and timeless art collection of J. J. Haverty
William Rawson Smith.—1st ed.
p. cm.
Includes bibliographical references and index.
ISBN-13: 978-0-86554-992-0 | ISBN-10: 0-86554-992-3 (hardback : alk. paper)
1. Haverty, J. J. (James Joseph), 1858-1939
2. Art–Collectors and collecting–Georgia–Atlanta–Biography
3. High Museum of Art
I. Title.
N5220.H32S65 2006 | 709.2–dc22 | 2006006617

Acknowledgments

For as long as I can remember, fragments of J. J. Haverty's art collection were a part of my life. Above the living room fireplace mantle in my parents' home was the Henry O. Tanner painting, *Flight into Egypt*. And there were others in the house where I was raised, including John Johansen's *The Grand Canal* and a landscape by Jonas Lie. On countless occasions, I walked past splendid canvases acquired during the 1920s and 1930s by my great grandfather, rarely pausing to reflect on their origins. When visiting relatives, I sometimes encountered other paintings of the distinct American school that Haverty collected. Following the tradition of J. J. Haverty, my uncle Rawson Haverty opened his home to family gatherings each year at Christmas. There, I was always struck by a pair of matching full-length portraits of J. J. and Clara Haverty. These stunning canvases by Charles Naegele present a haunting likeness of this distinguished couple, their steely blue eyes gazing over all who enter the dining room.

Over the years, as I visited the great museums in New York, Paris, and Chicago, I sometimes wondered about the Haverty Collection, much of which was donated to the High Museum by J. J. Haverty's descendants. As it turned out, the High Museum parted with many pieces of the collection, returning some to family members while retaining a core group of the choicest paintings along with a few sculptures. Although the High has chosen not to display the paintings donated by Haverty as a coherent collection, many of the individual works continue to augment the museum's permanent collection and are prominently displayed in different locations.

The idea of writing a book about the J. J. Haverty Collection occurred to me as I stumbled across some of his speeches kept on file in the Atlanta Art Association Collection at the Atlanta History Center. I had heard others who barely knew my great grandfather describe his soft-spoken temperament, and the Sunday afternoon open house exhibitions of art at Villa Clare were part of our family's lore. But after reading Haverty's speeches, letters, and newspaper clippings, this extraordinary man began to assume a more life-like shape in my mind. Here was the collector in his own voice talking about his ideas and passions, his vision for art as a necessity of life for everyone—rich and poor, black and white. I was struck by his methodical determination to bring a museum to Atlanta and the way his plans, starting with the Grand Central Exhibitions in 1924 and 1925, unfolded precisely as he envisioned with Mrs. High's donation of her home as a permanent institution of the arts. Clearly, J. J. Haverty was a man of lasting accomplishment, and the more I learned about him the more I became convinced that he was a worthy subject of a book.

In acknowledging those who supported me with this book project, I want to thank Marc Jolley of Mercer University Press for encouraging a vague concept from a stranger. I want to thank Barbara Keene for tolerating a rookie author and helping me to get through the process of marketing and selling this book. I am also grateful to Mercer University Press editor Kevin Manus for helping me work through some of the organizational challenges with a story that involves many dimensions—business, art, family, etc.—over a lifetime of eighty-one years.

Villa Clare would not have been possible without strong encouragement from Michael Shapiro, the director of the High Museum. Michael graciously invited me to breakfast back in fall 2002 and offered his enthusiastic endorsement and knowledgeable insight. I want to thank Paula Williams in the High Museum registrar's office for her courteous and professional fulfillment help in expertly reproducing paintings in the permanent collection. Former High Museum director Gudmund Vigtel was also kind enough to have lunch with me and share his recollections of the Haverty collection and art in general during a walk through of the galleries where he used to preside.

The executives at Haverty Furniture Company have also been supportive, and I want to thank my brother Clarence Smith, Tom Curran, and others in that organization for promptly helping me to secure photos and other information relevant to the story of their business's founder, J. J. Haverty. Former Haverty chairman and CEO Rawson Haverty, Sr., and his son Rawson Haverty, Jr., were kind enough to let me look at some of their personal files for this project. Thanks also to Michael Brubaker and the others on staff at the Atlanta History Center's Kenan Research Center for their help and patience in procuring letters, scrapbooks, ledgers, newspaper clips, and other research materials. In addition, Monsignor Thomas Kenny and the staff and volunteers at the Cathedral of Christ the King in Atlanta have provided valuable assistance and support in the research of this book.

My friend Frank Reiss, owner of A Capella Books in Atlanta has been a constant source of encouragement and insight as I have shepherded this book from concept to reality. The same is true for his cohort and our mutual friend, author Rodger Brown.

This book would not be possible without the first-hand recollections of Rawson Haverty, Sr., and Betty Haverty Smith, J. J. Haverty's grandchildren and my uncle and mother, respectively. They have carried the flame of J. J. Haverty's love for art over the years and were most generous with their time by sharing stories, reading early drafts of this manuscript, and offering helpful suggestions. Rawson Haverty for years represented the Haverty family in its dealings with the High Museum and his correspondences were very enlightening. I should also acknowledge that I borrowed heavily from Rawson Haverty's excellent book on the history of the Haverty family, *Ain't the Roses Sweet*.

Finally, my deepest and most heartfelt thanks go to my wife, the most talented writer in the family, Amy Bonesteel. Amy is a constant source of love and inspiration to me and I'm indebted to her for tolerating my distractions from our most important concern: the well-being and happiness of our three beautiful children.

Quest for Beauty

As a boy, he watched Sherman's men torch his family home and served at the altar of the priest who saved Atlanta's churches. As a man, he started the South's largest chain of furniture stores and assembled one of the finest collections of American art in his day. Along the way, he dropped out of high school, led efforts to establish Atlanta's High Museum of Art, and earned the title "Knight Commander of St. Gregory," the highest honor for a layman in the Catholic Church.

J. J. Haverty's remarkable story is in many ways the story of Atlanta's rise from the ashes of the Civil War to become the South's leading cultural and commercial city. Yet this self-made and relentlessly focused son of Irish immigrants was an anomaly. His life presents contradictions that only begin to illustrate the depth of a visionary yet little understood man.

Despite his lack of formal education, Haverty read avidly and became one of the South's most successful retailers, pioneering the method of selling on credit and taking his company public just before the crash of 1929. He grew up in a working-class home with few luxuries or refinements but pursued a lifelong quest to surround himself with beauty and culture. He led efforts to memorialize the Confederacy on Stone Mountain, yet he also patronized and collected the work of one of America's first great black painters, Henry O. Tanner.

During his eighty-one years, Haverty left a profound legacy in his hometown of Atlanta, including the company that still thrives more than 120 years after its founding; the fragments of his original art collection are still on display at the High Museum; and the Cathedral of Christ the King, which he helped found. But Haverty was not a man to dwell on his accomplishments. He did not write memoirs, and his letters generally were businesslike and concise, similar to the man who wrote them. Little has been published about J. J. Haverty other than a plaque on the wall at the High Museum that briefly describes the collection donated after his death.

Haverty's private life revolved almost exclusively around business, his wife and ten children, religion, and of course art. Like many executives of his era, his demeanor was formal—his wife Clara referred to him in public as "Mr. Haverty," and he wore a suit and tie without fail, even during family dinners. He took pride in his disciplined work habits. "Nobody ever died from hard work," he told a reporter on his seventy-ninth birthday, an occasion he marked by going to the office.[1] In photos, the bespectacled retailer usually appears tight-lipped and deadpan. With no exposure to fraternity-based social norms, he had little use for frivolity; he even quit playing golf after one frustrating attempt. But he enjoyed flashing his sharp wit in conversation and was not above tossing back a glass of Bourbon or two after a hard workday. A voracious reader, Haverty could hold forth on myriad topics—none more passionately than fine art, in particular the American paintings and sculptures that appealed to his strong sense of patriotism and his uncanny eye for beauty.

J. J. Haverty was drawn to art collecting late in life, and, as he did with all endeavors that attracted his full attention, he pursued the acquisition of paintings and sculpture with quiet but relentless intensity. He read art criticism and assembled probably the best collection in his day in the Southeast. In the more narrow field of American realist and Impressionist art, his collection was one of the best anywhere. Following his death and the donation of the bulk of his collection to Atlanta's High Museum of Art, curators did not always share Haverty's artistic tastes, which were considered too conservative during the post-World War II heyday of abstract expressionism and modernism. During the 1920s and 1930s when he was actively collecting, Haverty was especially fond of figurative paintings depicting family life, Impressionist-style landscapes, and mystical images of characters and scenes from the Bible. But despite some paintings that were posthumously determined to be of lesser quality, the vast majority of his collection to this day is considered superb, and the work has been more than vindicated by the passage of time. For an idea of what moved Haverty, study the haunting glow of *Etaples Fisher Folk* by Henry O. Tanner or the stunning depiction of the New York harbor by Jonas Lie in *Path of Gold* (both in the High Museum of Art).

Later in life, Haverty displayed his collection of more than 100 works in his Italian-style home on Peachtree Street (near the present Shepherd Center for Catastrophic Care). Villa Clare was named after his beloved wife Clara, who died in 1918. Eventually, his unmarried daughter, May, assumed social responsibilities for the Haverty family, which included management of the burgeoning art collection.

Art for J. J. Haverty was something to be shared. Much to May's consternation, he had an open-door policy at Villa Clare on most Sundays, when people off the street were welcome to drop by and enjoy the Haverty collection. When it came to the enjoyment of art, he was a populist, a man who relished the chance to share beauty. "To appreciate a painting or a piece of sculpture or a lovely building does not require technical knowledge, nor extensive education, nor long training," Haverty told an audience in Macon, Georgia, in March 1927. "One can enjoy beauty as it finds expression in these works of art without training and without being rich. In Europe the peasants are lovers of art; they not only appreciate it but they live it."[2]

Living in a tumultuous age, Haverty never forgot his father's humble roots as an Irish immigrant and railroad worker. As a firsthand witness to the Civil War and Reconstruction, he grew up in a world where misery and suffering were commonplace and material beauty was scarce. Philosophically, he was a lifelong follower of the aesthetic movement exemplified by Oscar Wilde, who in the 1880s delighted an audience in Atlanta that included a young J. J. Haverty. Like most others in his day, Haverty was strongly influenced by the powerful winds of change that uprooted much of the traditional American way of life between the end of the Civil War and the beginning of World War II. Intercontinental railroads, electric lights, the telephone, indoor plumbing, the automobile, and the airplane were only a few of the innovations at that time. The art world reflected change as well, with the emergence of impressionism, "Ash Can" realism, and abstract concepts.

As a student of the school of hard knocks, Haverty suffered his share of setbacks, but eventually he capitalized on the clamor and upheaval of his day, in large part through sheer savvy and perseverance. In the process, he joined the ranks of men who set Atlanta apart from other Southern cities, visionaries of the same era such as Henry Grady, Asa Candler, and Horace Bradley. Bradley, an artist himself, brought artists together for the Cotton States Exposition and never lived to see the realization of his dream for a museum in Atlanta. J. J. Haverty was fortunately able to play a pivotal role in establishing a permanent art museum in the city. In the process, he helped make Atlanta a more beautiful and vibrant place for generations of people who followed him.

This book gives an overview of Haverty's life and the environment that shaped it. Interspersed are images from his work and home life, and there is a catalogue of his art collection with reproductions and descriptions of some of the work now in the permanent collection of High Museum of Art in Atlanta.

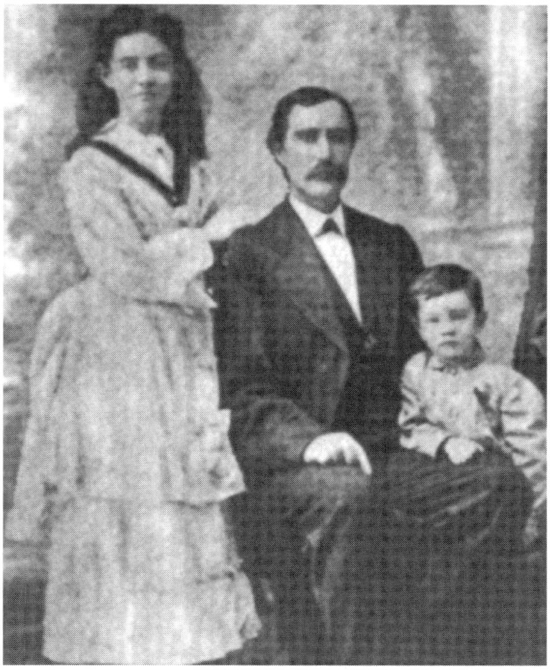

The earliest known picture of young J. J. Haverty, taken along with his father Thomas Haverty and his sister Ellen. Thomas Haverty left Ireland in 1848 and after settling in Atlanta brought over his family, including Ellen.

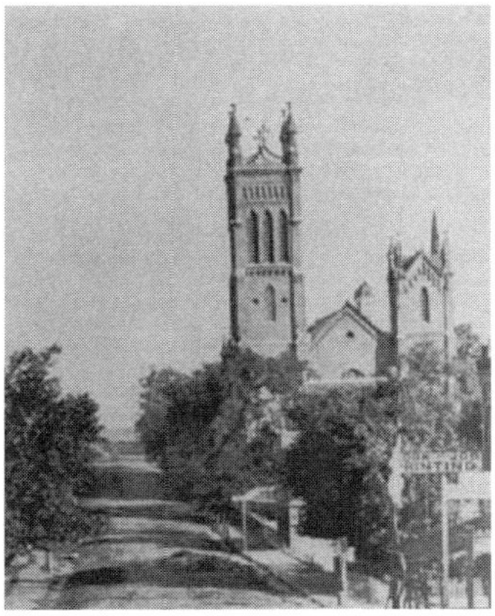

The Shrine of the Immaculate Conception as it appeared in 1873, now at 48 Martin Luther King Dr. in downtown Atlanta. During antebellum and Reconstruction era Atlanta, Immaculate Conception was at the center of life for the city's Irish community.

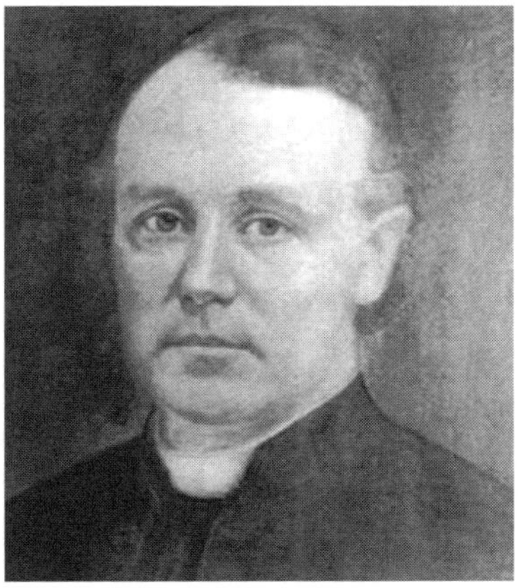

Haverty was an altar boy for Father Thomas O'Reilly, the Immaculate Conception priest who persuaded Union forces to spare Atlanta's three downtown churches and other essential property. O'Reilly's remains are preserved under glass in a crypt in the basement of the Immaculate Conception.

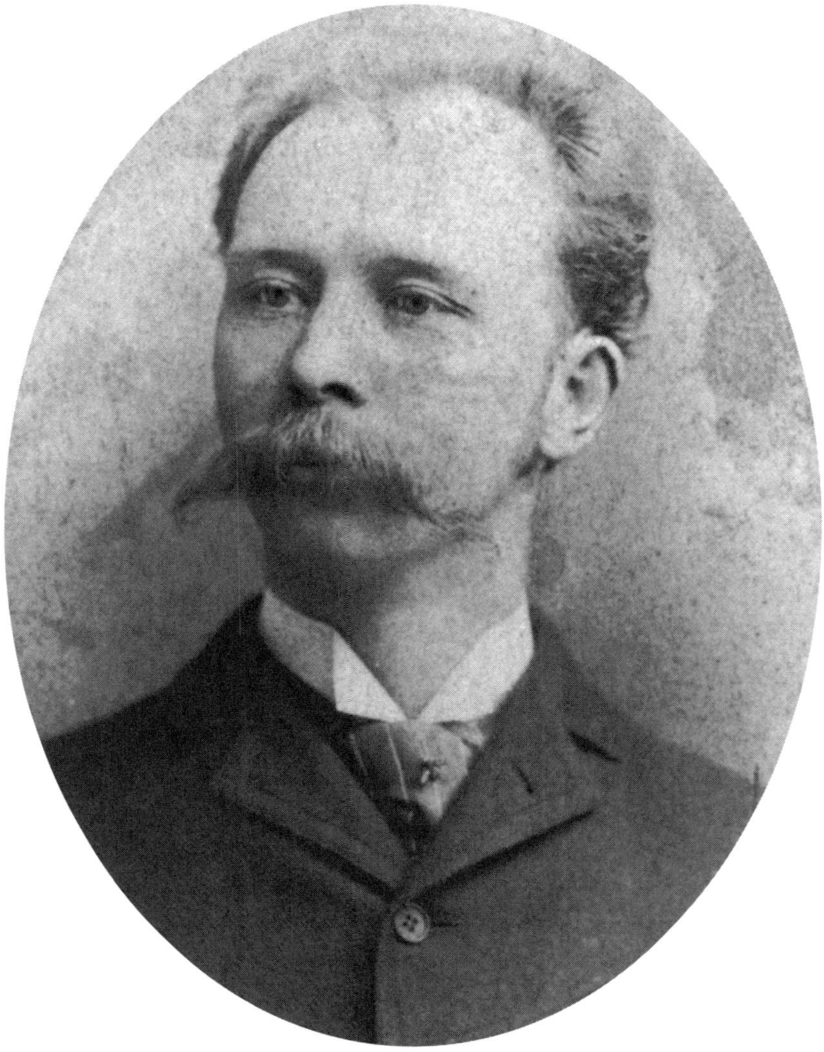

In the 1890s, a young J. J. Haverty sported the handlebar moustache popular in this era.

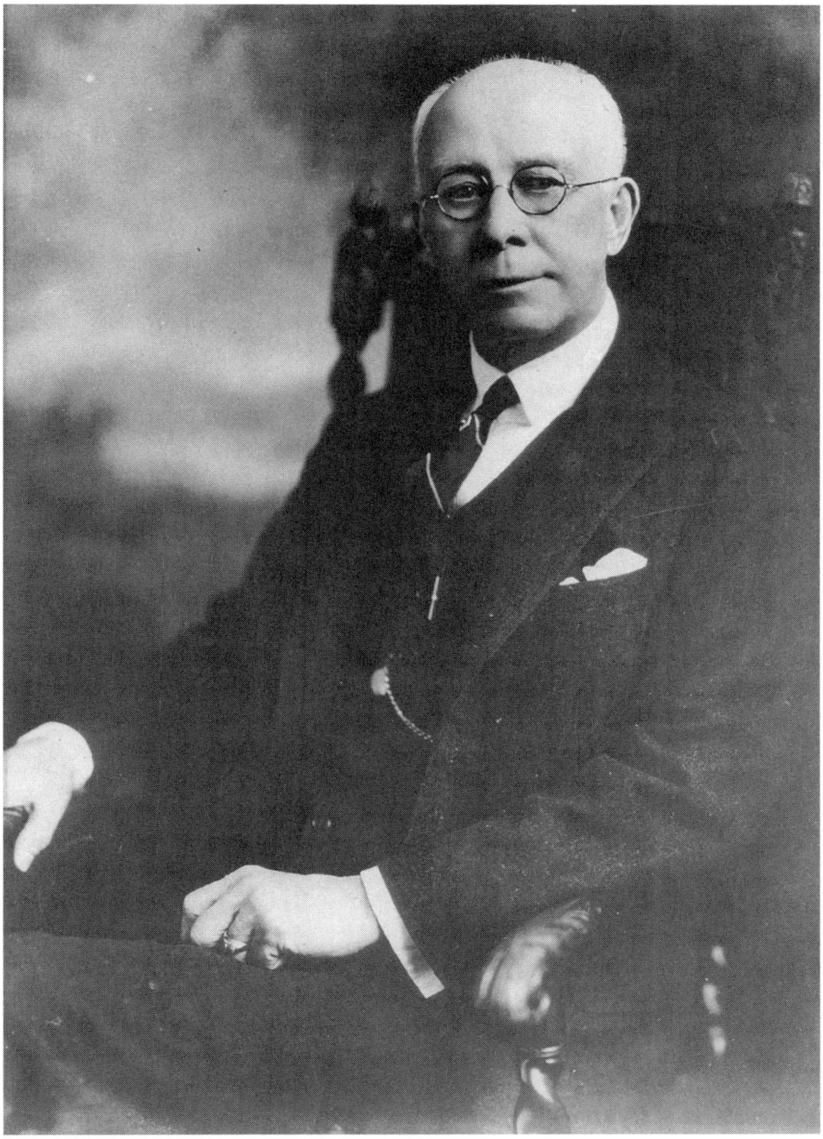

Haverty, wearing a pocket watch with chain, relaxes in his ornate office chair.

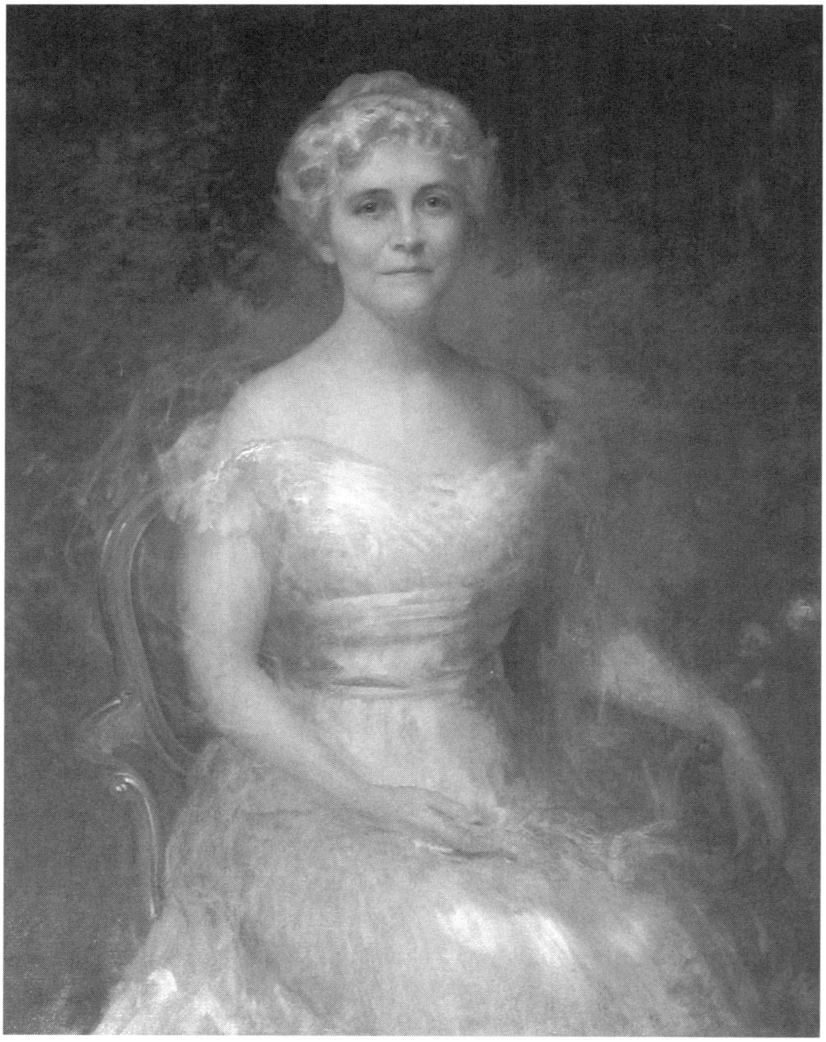

This pair of portraits by Charles Frederick Naegele depicts J. J. and Clara Haverty probably in their fifties.

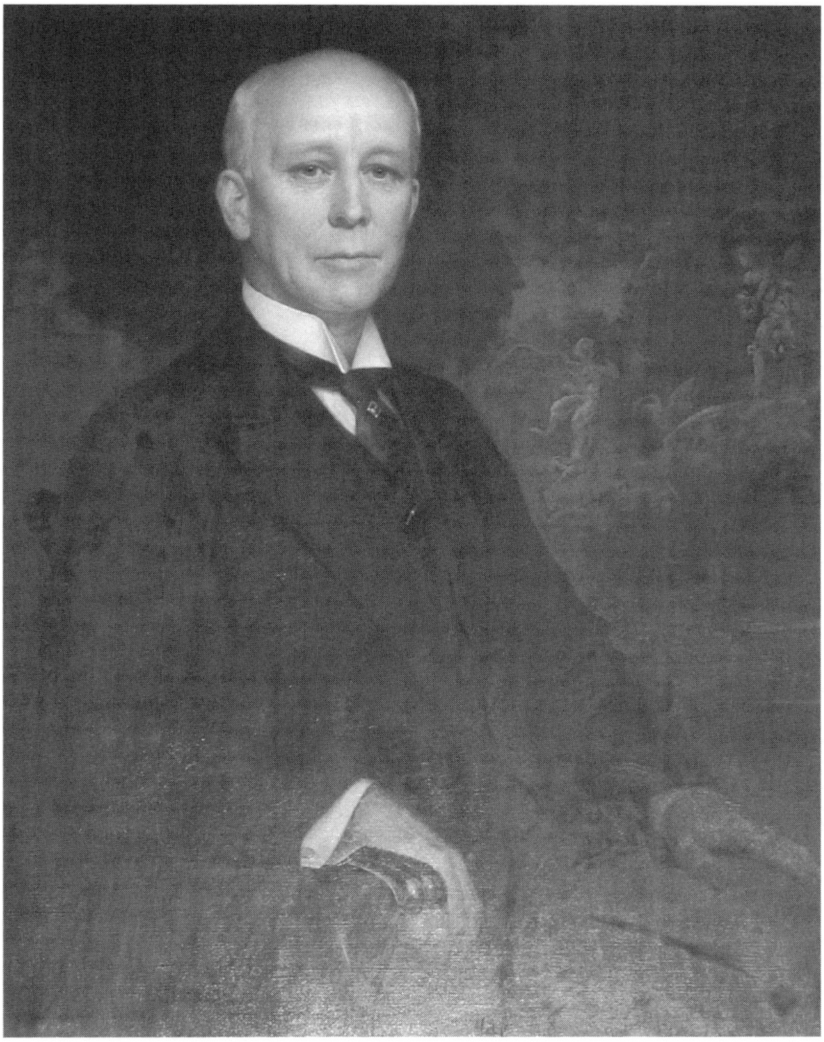

William Rawson Smith xix

During the 1920s, J. J. Haverty was one of Atlanta's most active civic leaders. He organized the Grand Central Exhibitions at the Biltmore Hotel in 1924 and 1925 while leading the Atlanta Art Association during the founding and early days of the High Museum.

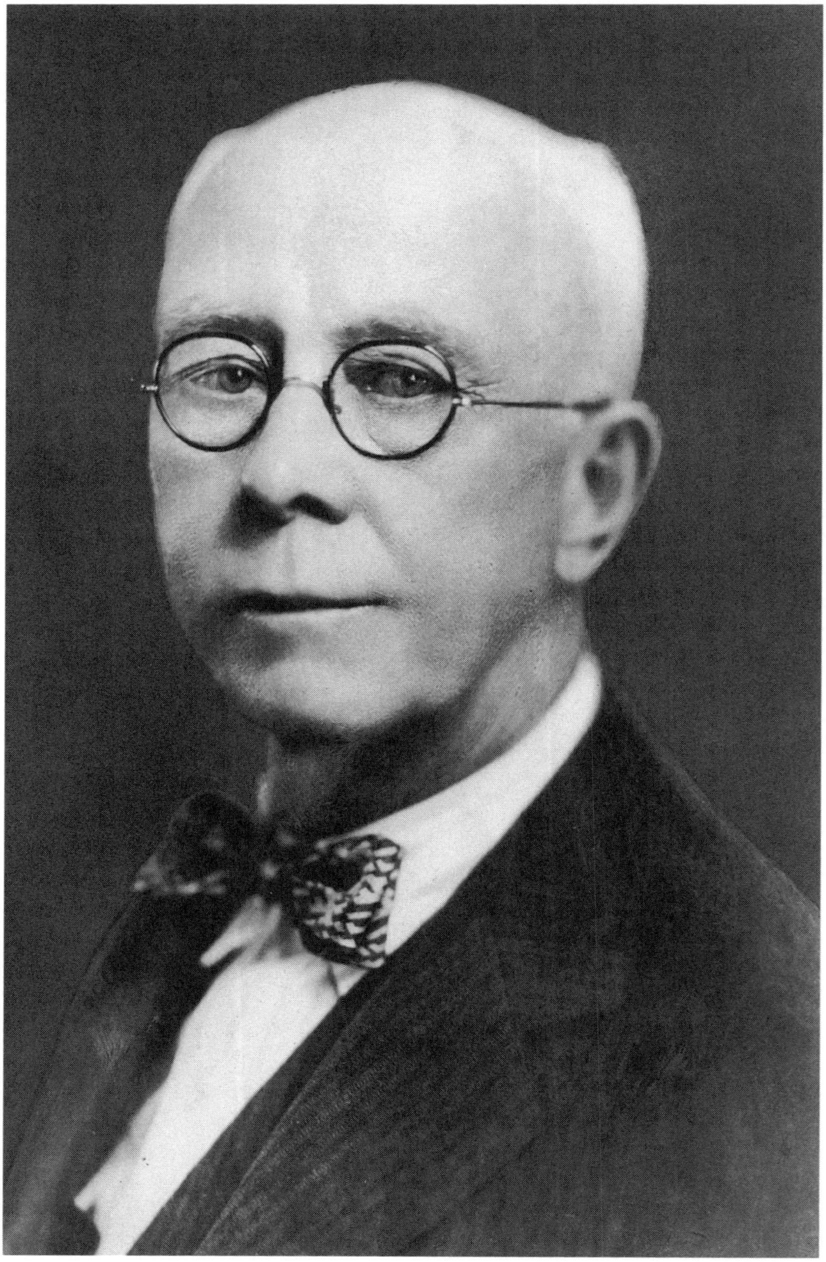

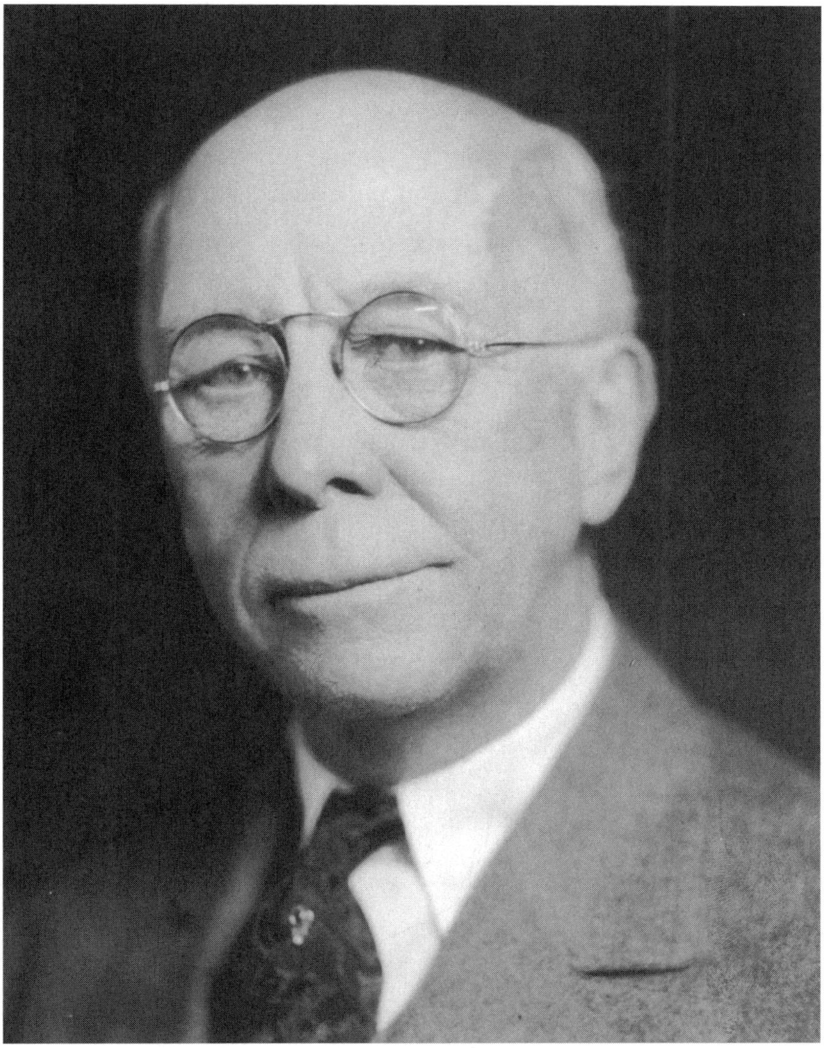

During the Depression, J. J. Haverty took advantage of the decline in the art market to pick up numerous bargains for his Villa Clare collection.

A catalogue of paintings and sculptures of Villa Clare. During the 1920s and 1930s, J. J. Haverty opened the doors of his home on Sunday afternoons to allow the public to enjoy his art collection.

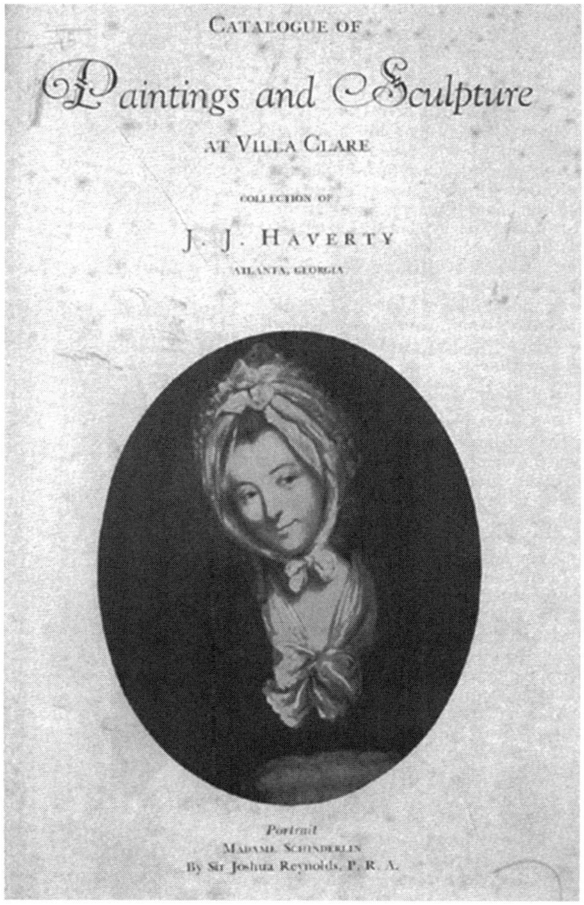

J. J. Haverty speaking to Bertram Newhouse of Newhouse Gallery in New York, a frequent source for paintings in the Villa Clare collection.

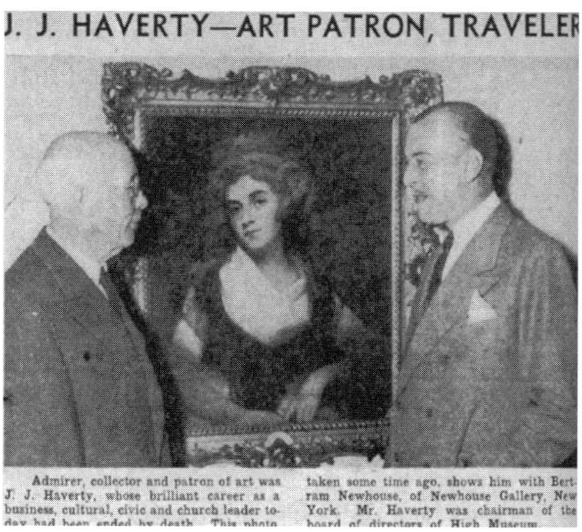
J. J. HAVERTY—ART PATRON, TRAVELER

Admirer, collector and patron of art was J. J. Haverty, whose brilliant career as a business, cultural, civic and church leader today had been ended by death. This photo taken some time ago, shows him with Bertram Newhouse, of Newhouse Gallery, New York. Mr. Haverty was chairman of the board of directors of High Museum.

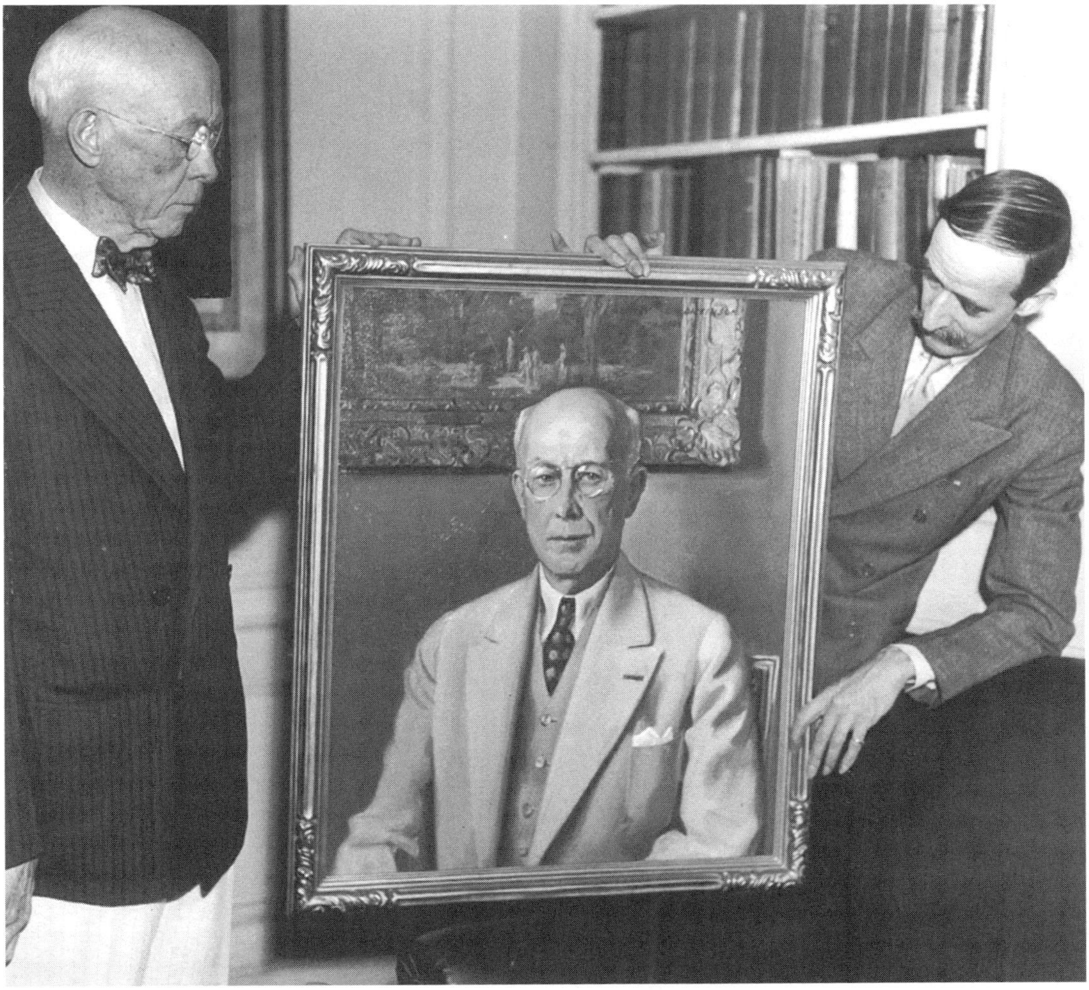

J. J. Haverty inspects a 1935 portrait by American painter Sidney Edward Dickinson, presumably the other man in the photo. In the background of this painting Dickinson depicts *Return of the Fishing Party* by J. Alden Weir, a painting purchased by Haverty and now in Atlanta's High Museum of Art

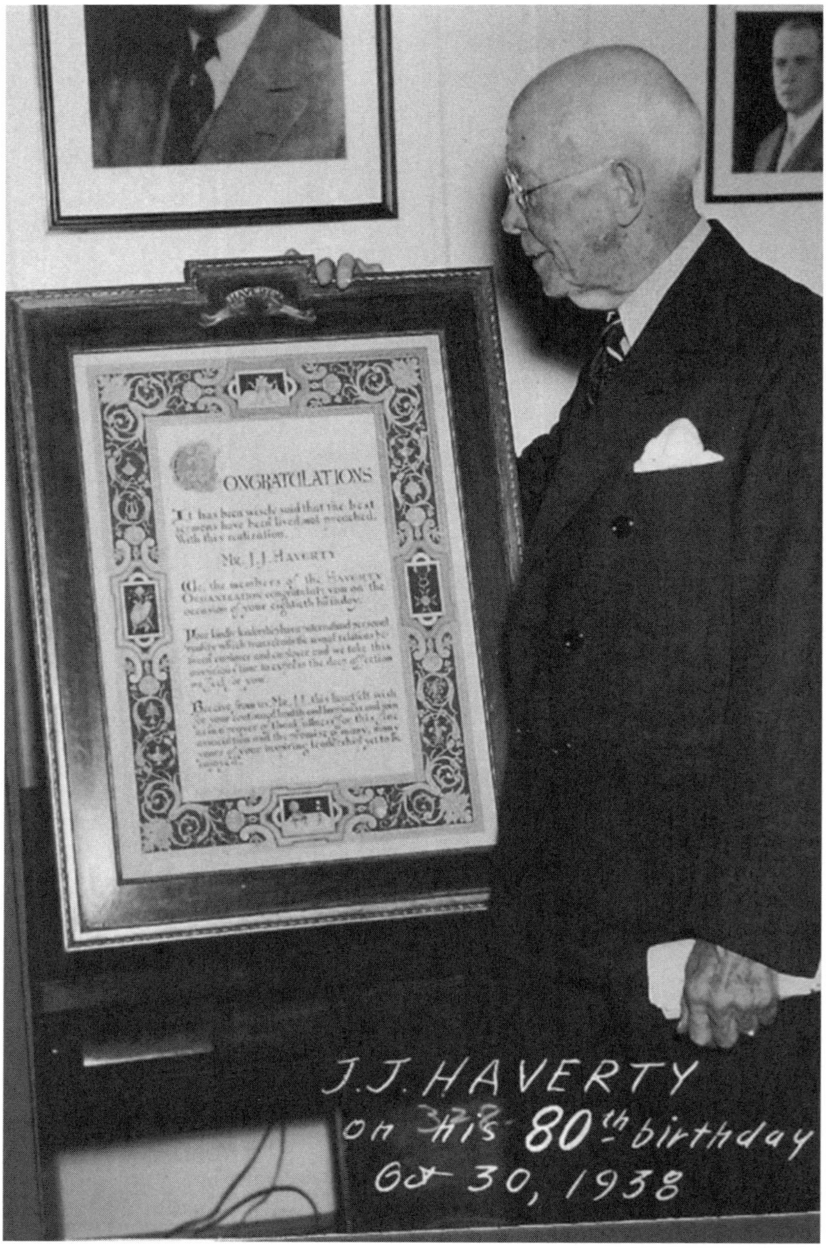

J. J. Haverty on the occasion of his eightieth birthday. Haverty is reading a plaque given to him by his coworkers, which begins, "It has been wisely said that the best sermons are lived and not preached..."

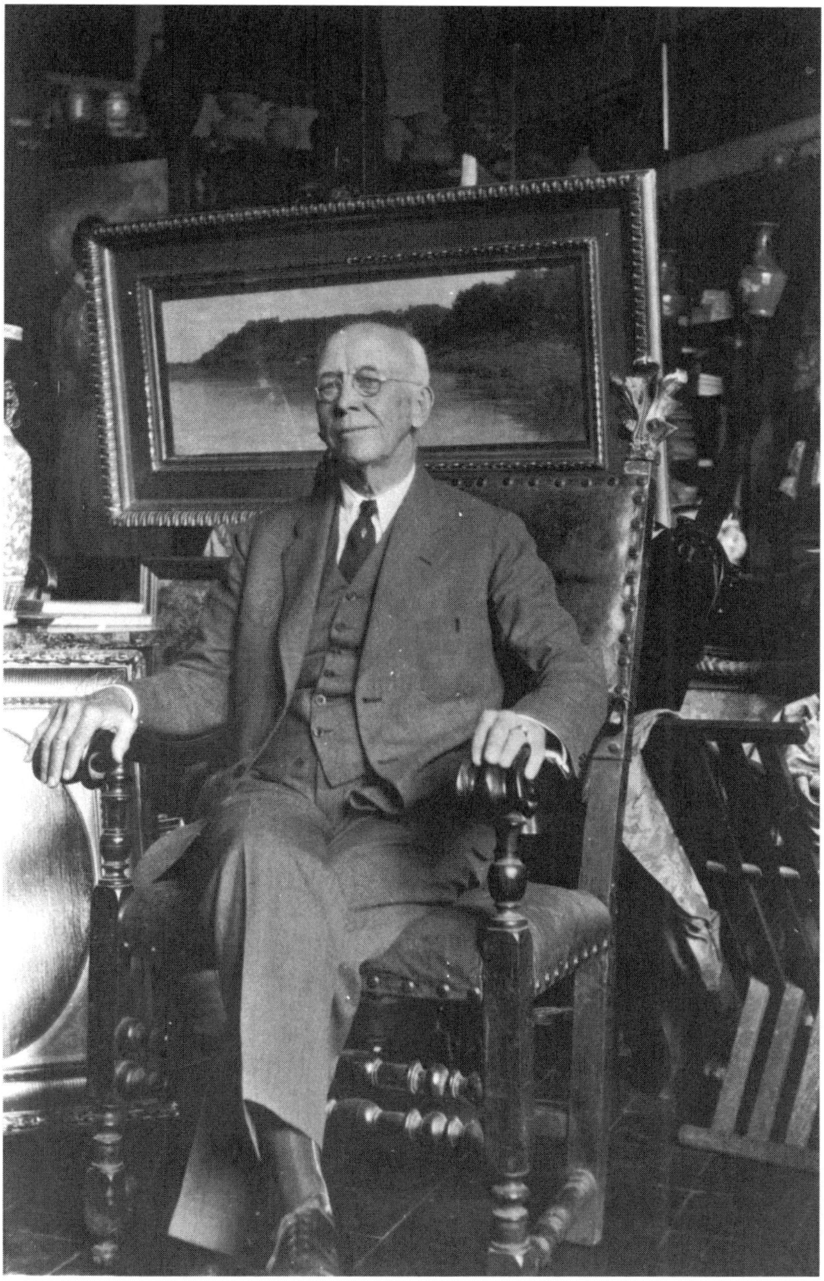

J. J. Haverty relaxes with artwork from his Villa Clare collection. "I know of no more intense passion, and I will add, no more beautiful passion, than the passion for the collecting of works of art," he said, quoting George Bernard Shaw.

Villa Clare

A Celt is notoriously a passionate, impulsive, kindly, unreflecting, brave, nimble-witted man; but he lacks the solidity, the balance, the judgment, the moral staying power of the Anglo-Saxon.

Atlantic Monthly, "The Irish in American Life," 1896

Welcome to the Gate City

Like millions of decent and hard-working Irishmen in the 1840s, Thomas Haverty confronted a world of stark alternatives. He lived in the Galway section of western Ireland, struggling to support a family amid a backdrop of low-level warfare between tribal warlords and increasingly vengeful British forces. At best, Haverty and the other Catholic inhabitants of Ireland were considered dubious subjects of the Protestant crown. Regardless of their qualifications, they were excluded from civil affairs and relegated to third-tier status as religious outcasts with little or no prospect for salvation, enlightenment, or even rehabilitation. With the king's handpicked lords in control of the island, ordinary natives were relegated to the most menial tasks, and many tried to make ends meet by coaxing potatoes, roots, or other edibles from parcels of rocky land.

By 1845, the misery worsened as a blight of black rot began to spread across the Irish countryside. With their crops dead or dying, tenant farmers begged landlords for a break. In reply, most of the Irishmen were told to pay up or get out. So millions of uprooted families wandered the island eating garbage and bugs—anything to get by. The weak, sick, and elderly were the first to die. Then children who were unwilling or too weak to beg or steal began falling by the wayside. Within five years, nearly a million people in Ireland had died from starvation. Another million, including many of the strongest and brightest, left the troubled island altogether.

One of the emigrants was Thomas Haverty, father of four young children.[3] Based on sketchy records, Haverty probably had better prospects than many of his countrymen. He had a decent education and married well. His father-in-law was a doctor. He claimed ancestry from the kings of Ireland. "His people, while of very modest circumstances financially, as was true of all the Irish people who came to America in those days, were substantial people in Ireland.... One of his uncles was Crown Counselor to Australia, under Queen Victoria,]another kinsman, Martin Haverty, the historian, was an authority on Irish history."[4] Whatever his prospects in Ireland, Thomas Haverty obviously perceived a better opportunity on the other side of the Atlantic. He left Ireland along with his older brother Stephen, who wound up taking a boat down the west coast of Africa, past the Cape and east to Australia.

Because there are no deep-water ports in Ireland, the trip to America started in the English port city of Liverpool. Haverty left in 1848, his destination the booming cotton port city of New Orleans. Virtually all of the Irish passengers at the time who took the route to New Orleans boarded cotton ships, providing lucrative ballast for the ship's return to port. This was the heyday of King Cotton, and the North Atlantic was packed with ships transporting raw cotton from the southeastern United States to British mills.

The voyage was miserable. Passengers were crowded under the main deck in filthy conditions for a treacherous ten-week trek. On the worst ships, it was not uncommon for many passengers to die en route, their bodies tossed overboard for an anonymous burial at sea.

As the rickety boats pitched and rolled across the Atlantic, the men and only a few women spent much of their time waiting in line for their turn to use a single stove on the main deck, weather permitting. When it rained, Haverty and the other passengers had to settle for eating raw flour or meal.

The opportunity that beckoned at the end of the voyage looked impressive, at least at a distance. After the United States secured access to California and the southwest in the Mexican War, vast spaces and fertile plains of North America were suddenly open to settlement. But as a practical matter, the road to prosperity in the New World was fraught with peril. Virtually all American cities in the middle of the nineteenth century were rowdy and dirty, with gas-lit streets covered not in gold but in mud, trash, and horse manure. The teaming neighborhoods were dangerous, crime-ridden places, and Irish immigrants occupied the worst slums. Anti-Irish violence was routine given that the Know-Nothing political and social movement thrived on a platform of immigrant bashing and anti-Catholicism.

Hostility was intense in the teeming tenements of New York and Baltimore. But the Irish were generally welcome in the South. Despite its humid and buggy climate, New Orleans was an alluring port of arrival. It was the largest city in the Southeast and strategically positioned as the primary gateway into the burgeoning Midwest. An influx of Irish laborers kept the port humming, and Haverty arrived in New Orleans in August 1848. But he did not stay long. He wanted as much money as he could get for his time and labor, and the standard rate for laborers was about $120 per year.

He headed northeast through the fertile, cotton-rich piedmonts of Mississippi and into the rugged foothills of the Appalachian Mountains. His destination was a rowdy railroad town in northwest Georgia at the connection of the Western & Atlantic line from Tennessee and the Macon and Georgia railroad leading to Savannah and Charleston. Haverty made Atlanta his base of operations and became a US citizen in 1852. During this milestone event, he was described as "about 30 years of age" with "blue eyes, light hair and fair complexion."[5]

Like most immigrants, Haverty went wherever he could find decent paying work. For a while, he took a construction job on the Shelbyville line of the Nashville & Chattanooga Railroad in Tennessee, working side by side with African-American laborers. Typically, the most dangerous and demanding work was assigned to the Irish, a hard-working but hot-blooded lot who were inclined to ease their drudgery with whiskey and fisticuffs. Using black powder and hand tools, Haverty's team bored 2,228 feet through Cumberland Mountain limestone and shale, an engineering wonder known as the Cowan Tunnel.[6]

Historians continue to marvel at the brutal conditions of nineteenth-century railroad workers.

> How hard they worked is an astonishment to us in the 21st Century.... Their hands were tough enough for any job—one never sees gloves in the photographs—which included pickax handling, shoveling, wielding sledgehammers, picking up iron rails and using other equipment that required hands of iron. Their waists were generally thin, but oh those shoulders! Those arms! Those legs! They were men who could move things, hammer things in and swing things, whatever was required, in rain or snow or high winds or burning sun and scorching temperature, all day, every day.... They didn't whine, they didn't complain they didn't quit, they just kept working.[7]

A New Home on the Tracks

After nearly a decade of brutal labor, Haverty finally had earned enough to send for his family.[8] His wife and four children moved from Ireland to Atlanta in 1857, and within a year another child was born. James Joseph Haverty grew up in a muddy, gas-lit slum crowded with gamblers, cockfighters, prostitutes, and violent criminals. The city's most notorious attraction was the Athenaeum Theater, where a rowdy audience pelted hapless performers with rotten fruit. Those who could not afford the price of admission could enjoy the spectacle of drunken brawls, jugglers, and freak shows on Humbug Square not far from the Havertys' home below the main train station, at the present site of Underground Atlanta.[9] One visitor said, "professed gamblers and 'filles de pave,' with a considerable sprinkling of pickpockets, horse thieves, and incendiaries, as spice to the condiment early Atlanta was populated primarily by 'whiskey dealers.'" Another summed up the rugged frontier town as a place for "stump speeches, barbecues and fisticuffs.... A rougher village I never saw."[10]

Atlanta was not like other Southern cities ruled by the planter class. The pine-covered hills were not fertile, and few residents owned slaves. In addition to red clay, North Georgia in the mid-nineteenth century offered gold and fast-moving streams to power productive mills and factories. Best of all were countless acres of wilderness abandoned after the forced exodus of the Cherokees in 1835. The entrance to this wild and dangerous land of opportunity was the Havertys' hometown of Atlanta—hence its nickname, the Gate City.

It was a new kind of city, open to change and oblivious to tradition. People of initiative and ambition were welcome, and pedigree was of relatively little concern. E. Y. Clarke wrote of Atlanta, "There is no city in this or any country more free from the domination of caste; admission to society being based on character alone.... All men are welcomed and eagerly welcomed to our midst—capitalist or laborer, the seeker after a home or employment—objection being made only to drones."[11]

The railroads were essential to early Atlanta's economy and identity. Hulking steam engines rumbled through the heart of the city at all hours, spewing sparks, belching foul smoke, jamming foot traffic, and disrupting life for downtown residents like the Havertys. City leaders begged the railroad operators to build bridges or viaducts where people could cross the lines. They also wanted land set aside in the heart of the city for a public park. The powerful vested interests were in no way bound to respond to these petty grievances. For years after Atlanta was founded, engines routinely crushed or maimed residents as the people tried to make their way across the treacherous tracks.

Commercially, the city brimmed with dash and verve. Factory laborers, railroad workers, dry goods merchants, snake oil salesmen, entertainers, bricklayers, and various men of the cloth found Atlanta to their liking and called it home. Upstart hustlers also found the city an excellent place to risk capital and turn a profit. Throughout its history, Atlanta has been kind to attorneys. There was no shortage of crime or disputes in the bustling seat of Fulton County, and the fast-growing base of local businesses provided ample demand for legal services. During its first two decades, the city's population climbed to 8,000 in 1856 with 75 businesses.

Even though Atlantans grew little of the crop, "King Cotton" was an indirect source of wealth in the Gate City. The price of cotton increased during the 1850s as textile factories in England and the northeast US began production. As the main depot and switching station for southbound supplies and northbound cotton, Atlanta was in an ideal place to capitalize on this booming trade. Progress was marked by the construction of a city hall, a medical college, a cotton warehouse, and the four-story Trout House hotel, the largest between Louisville and New Orleans.[12]

Torn Allegiances

Amid the mayhem of life in early Atlanta, the Shrine of the Immaculate Conception provided a sanctuary for people adjusting to a life as strangers in a strange land. Founded in 1848 by a group of missionaries passing through Georgia from Augusta and Savannah, the shrine before the Civil War was a square wooden box with an A-frame roof. Although the setting lacked grandeur, it was a place to hear familiar Latin verses and experience comforting rituals. Most of the members were, like the Havertys, working-class immigrants seeking to assimilate.[13]

After the election of President Abraham Lincoln in 1860, many Atlantans were ambivalent about the prospect of secession. The Havertys were typical in that they did not own slaves and were more concerned with business than firebrand politics. As a naturalized citizen, Thomas Haverty had sworn an oath to the US and had no grievance against his national government. He was like the majority of Atlantans who supported the anti-secession Democratic Party candidate during the election of 1860.[14]

But members of the younger generation typically had a different view of events and were more responsive to the call to arms. In 1861, J. J.'s brother Michael, who was seventeen years older, and brother-in-law Thomas Daly joined the Jackson Guards, officially known as Company B of the 19th Regiment of the Georgia Volunteer Infantry. Serving under Colonel Thomas C. Johnson, this Confederate Army unit fought in Virginia, Florida, and South Carolina and eventually surrendered at the end of the war in North Carolina. With the rank of 3rd sergeant, Michael Haverty had a reputation as a raconteur, and his letters were eagerly anticipated. As Thomas and his family relaxed in the candlelit parlor in Atlanta, young J. J. listened eagerly as his parents read firsthand accounts of epic battles from the Virginia theater in West Point, Seven Pines, Mechanicsville, Gaines Mill, Frazier's Farm, and Malvern Hill.[15]

During the early part of the war, Atlanta prospered as soldiers and supplies poured through the city. But the horrors of combat became all too real in North Georgia after General William T. Sherman invaded in early 1864. The Union's huge triple army fought and flanked its way south through the mountains from Chattanooga and by July had crossed the Chattahoochee River, the last natural obstacle to the "Gate City." As guns roared in the distance and wounded soldiers entered the city in ever-growing numbers, nerves began to fray. Union forces routed counterattacking rebels at Peachtree Creek and Ezra Church, forcing the battered Army of Tennessee to retreat inside the fortified city. Sherman surrounded Atlanta in early August and for weeks rained shells on the downtown area where the Havertys lived. Along with other terrified families, they hunkered down in makeshift basements, trying to avoid random death from Union cannon fire.

Late in August, Sherman isolated Atlanta with a massive flanking attack at Jonesboro that severed the city's remaining rail link. Confederate general John B. Hood had little choice but to order the defending soldiers to evacuate Atlanta under cover of darkness. On the way out, Hood started the first burning of Atlanta. His men torched a long train of railroad cars full of supplies and ammo, sparking blasts that demolished the rail yard and rained ordinance for miles around the city.

Although J. J. Haverty was only six at the time, he recalled the frightening spectacle in vivid detail years later. In the words of teenage diarist Mary Rawson, "On arising a most beautiful spectacle greeted our sight. The Heavens were in a perfect glow while the atmosphere seemed full of flaming rockets, crash follows crash and the swift moving locomotives were rent in pieces and the never tiring metallic horse law powerless while the sparks filled the air with innumerable spangles."[16]

The next morning on 1 September, Atlanta's mayor and a few council members rode out of the smoldering city to contact Union troops and gain favorable terms for surrender. They made a good impression but received little if anything in return for their gesture of appeasement. By noon, the US flag was flying from the landmark Trout House in downtown Atlanta, and Union supply wagons were moving into the conquered city.

The Priest and the General

Fearing the worst, residents peeked from behind drawn curtains to watch the conquering Yankees. Among the first to greet them was Father Thomas O'Reilly, the feisty Irish pastor of the Shrine of Immaculate Conception and a mentor to young J. J. Haverty. O'Reilly was an official Confederate chaplain who had distinguished himself by caring for wounded rebels in Newnan, Marietta, and LaGrange.

During the Battle of Atlanta, he was among a handful who offered to help some 40,000 wounded soldiers and civilians. At the peak of the Atlanta campaign, rows of wounded men were sprawled on makeshift cots or floors in churches, parks, homes, and hospitals across town. Father O'Reilly "is a highly educated gentleman, and a Christian in every sense of the word, and we feel and know he would discharge the duties of the position he desires with the greatest alacrity and promptness," wrote a Confederate officer in a letter to the war secretary in Richmond recommending O'Reilly's designation as an official chaplain.

When Union troops brought their casualties into the city, O'Reilly made no distinctions, caring for all of the soldiers with no regard for uniform or rank. Many of Sherman's troops were Catholics—mostly from midwestern states—and after the fall of Atlanta O'Reilly invited them all to attend his parish. The road to reconciliation between North and South started in the pews of Immaculate Conception, with young J. J. Haverty serving at the altar. The Havertys and other local Catholics worshiped side by side with Union soldiers, taking communion from the same chalice. Inside the shell-damaged parish, the priest built a strong rapport with the "Fighting Irish" of the Union Army. Because of his respect and credibility, he was able to gain countless small liberties for residents during the occupation. "Father O'Reilly was constantly at work urging and obtaining favors from the Federal army of occupation, ameliorating in a hundred ways the condition of the captured city and its inhabitants."[17]

But Sherman was determined to "make Atlanta howl." In November 1864, O'Reilly heard about the general's secret plan to evacuate Atlanta and burn the entire city to the ground, and he demanded an audience with the Union commander. Sherman had no use for O'Reilly and even considered having him executed for treason. But the Union commander knew that drastic option would cause problems in his ranks.[18] The priest was able to meet with US general Henry Warner Slocum, an attorney from New York who commanded Sherman's left wing. Wearing full-length black vestments and speaking in a thick Irish brogue, O'Reilly appealed for mercy and suggested that the Irish soldiers in blue might mutiny if Sherman went ahead with his plans for complete destruction. Eventually, the two men agreed on a compromise—the Union soldiers would move ahead with plans to burn the residential and commercial portions of the city but would spare the shrine and three other Atlanta churches, along with key government buildings that contained municipal records. "Under the representations of the priest, a guard was stationed about all the adjacent property and violence forbidden against the City Hall, the Catholic Church, the Second Baptist, the Central Presbyterian, Trinity Methodist and St. Philip's Episcopal, all residences included within the area of Loyd and Washington, Mitchell and the Railroad being immune from the torch of cannonade."

A few blocks away, the Haverty family lived in a modest row house near the main train station. They had nowhere to go as Sherman's men calmly went about the business of torching Atlanta. As a seven-year-old boy, J. J. Haverty never forgot the day soldiers knocked on his front door and sheepishly proceeded to burn his family home to the ground. "They were very polite about it," J. J. told his grandchildren years later during a Sunday afternoon family luncheon at his home on Peachtree Street. "The Union soldiers apologized for what they were doing and explained they were only following orders. They rolled up newspapers, placed them under the family staircase, and calmly proceeded to set the place on fire."[19]

With the arrival of winter, the entire city was homeless. In a city of about 10,000 people, Sherman's forces destroyed some 4,000 to 5,000 buildings, according to Confederate general W. P. Howard, who inspected Atlanta in late November 1864. Sherman's aide-de-camp, Major Ward Nichols, described the "grand and awful spectacle" of a

> beautiful city now in flames.... The heaven is one expanse of lurid fire; the air is filled with flying, burning cinders; buildings covering two hundred acres are in ruins or in flames; every instant there is the sharp detonation or the smothered booming sound of exploding shells and powder, concealed in the buildings, and then

> the sparks and flame shoot away up into the black red roof, scattering cinders far and wide.[20]

The people returned to squalid conditions. Orphaned children wandered the rubble-strewn and muddy streets looking for parents. Wild animals roamed unchecked, picking through all manner of debris. Small pox and other diseases were rampant. Rogues and deserters preyed on the weak, looting and robbing at will. The destitute squatted in makeshift Federal tent cities or abandoned Confederate breastworks.

Confronted with such bleak prospects, many Southerners turned inward, nurturing a sense of bitterness and hostility. The Havertys, along with many other Atlantans, appeared to have a different attitude toward Reconstruction. They put the war behind them and decided to get back to work, aiming to make the most of the small opportunities in front of them instead of dwelling on the death and destruction everywhere around them.

Atlanta Resurges

A key player in Atlanta's reconstruction was Father O'Reilly. He managed to rebuild his war-damaged parish on a far bigger scale after the war. He also led efforts to help the legions of Atlanta's post-war needy. Parish members found a support network, food, medical attention, and a semblance of shelter. The Havertys lost their house for a while, but they always had a place to go at the shrine.

The return of the eldest son Michael after the end of the Civil War gave the family reason to celebrate. Michael had survived years of brutal fighting in the Virginia theater and a stint in a Union prisoner of war camp. When he returned to Atlanta, he received a hero's welcome. The hardscrabble veteran quickly settled down and married Alicia O'Brien. Trying to support a family during the reconstruction, Michael and his father found work as gardeners. Thomas had few skills and a weak back, but he did not mind the relatively mild labor of maintaining lawns and yards for his more affluent neighbors.

Michael had a different view. He had little use for yard work and instead decided to go into business with his old army buddy, Martin Daly. The two men opened the Haverty & Daly Shamrock Saloon, a friendly place to enjoy a taste of grog and camaraderie. It was not a bad career move. In many ways, the saloon keeper was a step up on the social ladder from the laborer, or in Michael's case the soldier. But the business of running a bar in the nineteenth century was not for the faint of heart. Beggars and thieves crowded the streets outside along with entertainers and salesmen, such as a smooth-talking, silk-hat-sporting character known simply as "Jones." Working under the glow of kerosene torches, Jones made a living hawking benzene soap in Atlanta's Humbug Square after the Civil War and worked in tandem with Lad Williams, a bearded violinist and banjo player.

Characters who could have been torn from the pages of *Huckleberry Finn* colored the world of J. J.'s youth and may have contributed to his lackluster academic career. J. J. attended public schools and Walpole's Private School, one of the first parochial schools in Atlanta. But his recollections were not favorable. Years later he told his daughter Margaret that his most vivid memory of school was when his professor "whipped me, and I didn't deserve it."[21]

But Haverty had a keen eye, and he noticed opportunity crackling across his hometown. Boosters coined the name "Phoenix City," comparing Atlanta to the mythological Greek bird that rose from the ashes, and they changed the city's seal to reflect the new image. "The narrow and irregular streets are alive from morning till night with draws and carts and hand-barrows and wagons," wrote a Chicago newspaper correspondent while describing Atlanta in 1865.Everywhere he went in Atlanta, the newspaperman encountered

> hauling teams and shouting men, with loads of lumber and loads of brick and loads of sand with piles of furniture and hundreds of packed boxes with mortar makers and hog carriers—with carpenters and masons, with rubbish removers and house-builders,

> with never ending throng of pushing and crowding and scrambling and eager and excited and enterprising men, all bent on building and trading and swift fortune making.[22]

Amid this bustle, clever and hard-working men often were able to land a job, if they were willing to start at the bottom and show initiative and loyalty. J. J. Haverty possessed ample quantities of these attributes. In 1872 at age fourteen, he found employment as a "cash boy" for Ryan's, a department store in downtown Atlanta. Haverty worked hard, earned the trust of the boss, and after a short time moved up to the position of clerk. A gruff self-made Irishman, Ryan took a liking to his enthusiastic retail apprentice.

As a practical lad, Haverty weighed the benefits of collecting a steady paycheck and striking up conversations with lady shoppers against the alternative of drawing lashes from a schoolmaster. He came to the not irrational conclusion that the former was a better way to live. Although his parents urged him to continue his studies, Haverty steadily worked his way up through the ranks at Ryan's and eventually dropped out of school. He was an avid reader and an immensely curious young man. It was in this capacity as a retail clerk that he went to the "school of hard knocks" to learn about business and art and the changes unfolding beyond Atlanta.

When Thomas Haverty watched his teenaged son going off to work at as a clerk, he was reminded of why he chose to leave Ireland and come to America in the first place. In his own way, Thomas Haverty had found the American dream. He established a new life in a new land starting with nothing but a strong back and a willingness to work. Now, only twenty years after his arrival, his youngest son was prospering as a merchant, using his wits instead of his brawn and rising several rungs above laborer on the social hierarchy. The new generation of the Haverty family was off to a good start.

We spend our days, each one of us, in looking for the secret of life. Well, the secret of life is in Art.

Oscar Wilde, 1882

Art and the Age of Expositions

While working as a retail clerk at Atlanta's Ryan's department store during the 1870s, J. J. Haverty had a unique window into a rapidly changing world. He watched with fascination as powerful trends reshaped not only the American household, but also the entire economy. During the antebellum years, only upper-crust elites could afford decent amenities for the home. Indoor plumbing was rare, and luxuries from plush furnishings to rugs to pianos were seen in only the finest homes. Quality items were typically scarce and expensive because they were made by hand and difficult to transport. But change occurred quickly with the emergence of steam-powered transportation and electronic communications. Factories, transportation methods, and financial markets around the world became automated and linked together in a vast network of commerce. As a result, prices of many consumer goods plunged, and millions of young families were able to afford amazing and ingenious items that their ancestors could not even imagine. The great American middle class had arrived.

Haverty kept close tabs on these changes through casual conversations with customers, mostly ladies. Since he rang up the sales in the interior department, he had his finger on the pulse of the consumer, and he noticed a rise in demand for decorative products. Along with the rush to upgrade the home, something else was happening: people began talking more about lofty topics such as "high art" and "aesthetics."[23] Even though times were tough after the recession of 1873, a new generation made great efforts to distinguish themselves by acquiring and displaying items of fine taste. If they could not afford elegant new furniture, they at least wanted to know about it and be able to discuss it intelligently. Most people assumed their prospects would improve and soon they would be able to enjoy the finer things in modern American life.

This new zeitgeist of the late Victorian era was known as the "aesthetic" movement, which was an extension of the "arts and crafts" movement begun by designer William Morris in Great Britain in the 1850s. The basic idea of aesthetics was that good taste and appreciation of beauty should be instilled in the general public. It took a while for this movement to filter down to Atlanta and the country's less-populated outposts, but thanks to new mass-circulation magazines and catalogues, ideas spread within a few years instead of decades. Merchants such as Haverty's boss, Ryan, were only happy to fuel the trend by marketing aesthetic furnishings and other decorative items. They published eye-catching ads to motivate consumers to upgrade their interiors and display good taste. J. J. Haverty, the curious young man who charmed the lady customers and handled the cash at Ryan's, became a self-taught student of aesthetics. He wanted to learn more, and in summer 1876 he got his chance.

Philadelphia Hosts the World

The Centennial Exhibition in Philadelphia took place from May to November 1876, covering 450 acres in Fairmount Park at a cost of nearly $11 million.[24] Some 9 million people in a nation of 46 million—1 in every 5—attended the festivities thrown to mark America's 100th birthday.

Despite the recession taking place at this time, promoters were determined to set a new standard for excellence in the age of expositions. London dazzled the world with the Crystal Palace Exposition in 1851, and Paris upped the stakes with a lavish display of French culture at L'Exposition Universelle in 1867. European elites considered New York's Crystal Palace show in 1853 a weak imitation of the British version, and many were doubtful as Philadelphia prepared for its chance to host the world, barely a decade after the end of America's Civil War.

Word about the exhibition traveled slowly during the infancy of mass media. Once Haverty heard about it, he quickly decided he wanted to attend, despite the difficulty of the journey. But even as a youth, he showed plenty of determination and resourcefulness, traits that would serve him well throughout his life. Haverty talked Mr. Ryan into giving him a leave of absence for several months and then persuaded other Southerners who were going to the exhibition to let him tag along. Sometime early in the summer, he scraped together enough money to buy a ticket north and set out for Philadelphia.

Atlanta after the Civil War was a largely forgotten backwater accessible only through the rickety Western & Atlantic rail line. The trip from Atlanta to Philadelphia started as a reverse of Sherman's March. The train left Atlanta and headed north through Allatoona and the Appalachian foothills to Chattanooga, then over the Tennessee River to Nashville, through Kentucky, and across the Ohio River. Cincinnati was about the halfway point. From there, the train headed due east toward the nation's population and industrial centers along the Atlantic Coast.

Haverty's destination, Philadelphia, certainly had plenty to offer an untraveled teenager. In the middle of the nineteenth century,

Philadelphians tended to look down on rival New York and its teeming slums. Although their city was no longer the nation's largest, residents of the city of brotherly love took pride in their refinement and quality of life. The city's fathers considered their home a silk-stocking refuge, site of the nation's first art museum with a reputation as the nation's premier cultural destination.

Although he later told family members his experience in Philadelphia made a profound impression, Haverty did not leave a record of his trip to the exhibition. He talked his way into a temporary job working for a southern textile company as a night watchman, working from 4:00 A.M. to 2:00 P.M. "My spare time was spent in the art exhibit and listening to Gilmore's Band," he wrote.[25]

In many ways, the exhibition was a microcosm of change in American society, and as an astute observer, Haverty likely appreciated its significance. For the citizens of a largely agrarian nation still recovering from the trauma of a conflict that left nearly half a million dead, it was an opportunity to heal old wounds and a chance for the people to come together and enjoy progress, art, and technology in a spirit of friendship and goodwill. The event seemed to mark America's entry into the exclusive ranks of powerful nations. It was an uneasy transition for many. As immigrants—increasingly from eastern and southern Europe—poured into cities to work in the bustling factories, millions of others set out on the arduous migration west. In the teeming cities back east, scientists were making technological breakthroughs at an astonishing pace. Hard-nosed and thick-skinned businessmen exploited cheap labor and innovation to build vast fortunes. For the first time, railroads and telegraph wires connected the country from coast to coast. New towns were born and others died. The sleepy land of rural hamlets and manual laborers that had attracted Thomas Haverty some three decades earlier had disappeared forever.

Given the nation's mindset toward progress, it's probably fitting that the star of the Centennial Exhibition was not a man but a machine. The Double Corliss Engine was a monstrous steam-powered contraption that hissed and churned to generate power for the vast Machinery Hall. In an elaborate ceremony opening the exhibition with 150,000 people on hand, President Ulysses Grant and Emperor Dom Pedro of Brazil cranked up the 56-ton machine in which two cylinders turned a 30-foot flywheel. Visitors were in awe of its size and output: 1,400 horsepower—the same as about five modern-day sport utility vehicles.[26]

America's steam-powered industrial prowess was evident throughout the exhibition, amazing even the most jaded visitors. But even with this impressive display of machinery, many Europeans left the exposition convinced of their own cultural superiority. When they saw the artistic and efforts set forth by uncouth upstarts on the west side of the Atlantic, cultural elites generally yawned. Indeed, much of the work lacked soul and seemed to be a poor imitation of European art. At a time when America's inferiority complex was pervasive, organizers of the exposition had a chip on their shoulder, and critics had a field day blasting the "vulgar" aspects of the event.

"It would be a barren place without the machinery," wrote one critic, who nevertheless expressed admiration for the "national genius" of "iron and steel." Others derided the haphazard setting of grandiose buildings surrounded by mud-caked fields, and the unwashed sea of humanity repulsed more than a few in attendance. "Much typhoid is caught there, and if they are not lucky they will have yellow fever," wrote visitor Henry Adams. Russell Lyons, author of the Tastemakers, went so far as to describe the exhibition as "an artistic calamity that produced not a single new idea but was, rather, the epitome of accumulated bad taste of the era that was called the Gilded Age, the Tragic Era, the Dreadful Decade, or the Pragmatic Acquiescence, depending on which epithet you thought most searing." [27]

But the exhibition was geared to the masses and not the critics. It was a patriotic affair, and many visitors who had been scarred by the Civil War were stirred by its symbolic unity and harmony. "No one can see the fair without a thrill of patriotic pride," wrote William Dean Howells.

Architect Joseph M. Wilson described the utopian vision of civilized diversity that he sought to create:

> The Main Building is one blaze of light, of flaming fire, from end to end owing to the reflections on the glass of the rays from the departing sun. It is a grand illumination. In the foreground the fountain has ceased to play, and the now quiet lake, a bright gem in its green setting, reflects every line and flash: The dome of Memorial Hall looks up over the trees—restless happy crows are flitting from point to point, and the whole pace looks like a fairy-land, an incantation scene, something that we wish would never pass away.

As an enthusiastic and wide-eyed youth, Haverty later told friends and family that he was dazzled by most everything he saw. Audiences were drawn by fantastic parades and displays of giant vegetables and farm animals, and there were unforgettable exhibitions, such as the colossal hand and torch designed by Italian sculptor Frederic Bartholdi. At a kiosk to raise money and promote the concept of the Statue of Liberty, visitors were offered brochures about Bartholdi's plan and were urged to buy subscriptions of as little as ten cents to help pay for the statue's pedestal.

The quantity of art was overwhelming even if the quality was inconsistent. The Italians set forth Roman-style marble busts and sculpture in abundance. Dutch exhibited what appeared to be thousands of dark and moody paintings of the Rembrandt style. French salons were rich with colorful works dedicated to the brilliance of Napoleon and the glory of *la culture Francaise*. The British were generous in their display of lovely green landscapes and depictions of the sea. Most astonishing to many were the exquisite and detailed watercolors from Japan.

Haverty enjoyed these displays from around the world, but the works of American artists particularly moved him. The Americans at this point did not have a particular school or even a real point of view, except to say that their work was derived from Europe. Many of the most talented artists, including James Whistler, studied and worked overseas. However, at the Centennial Exhibition a distinct American approach to painting first began to flicker, and exceptional works were on display. For instance, Thomas Eakins, the American realist pioneer who headed a rigorous European-style curriculum at the Philadelphia Academy in the 1870s, exhibited five paintings at the exhibition. The most famous was *Gross Clinic*, a painting of a surgical procedure that was initially rejected because of its bloody realism.[28]

Eakins was a mentor to many leading American artists of the late 1800s, including several African Americans. For instance, he taught Edward Mitchell Bannister, whose *Under the Oaks* was awarded one of four first-place prize medals at the Centennial Exhibition and was considered the best effort possible from an American artist. Bannister's techniques strongly influenced Henry O. Tanner, another of Eakins's students who attended the exhibition as a visitor. J. J. Haverty later collected Tanner's work and considered him one of his favorite artists. Other American artists exhibited at the Philadelphia Centennial Exhibition included talents still widely recognized and acclaimed, such as Gilbert Stuart, John Singleton Copley, and Winslow Homer.

The exhibition ended in November, but its legacy continued long after the Corliss engine stopped churning and the exhibitors packed their wares. Memorial Hall reopened as the Museum of Art and Industry, modeled on the Victoria & Albert Museum of London. In 1876, with help from local governments, Philadelphia also established a related school of industrial art to foster art and textile industries across Pennsylvania.[29] The school and museum were closely intertwined, providing the nation's first true institution for the visual arts and the inspiration for similar endeavors elsewhere. Many of the artworks found their way to the Smithsonian Museum in Washington. Other cities seethed with jealousy at Philadelphia's triumph and quickly mobilized efforts to compete. New York, Cincinnati, Chicago, and Boston quickly followed suit and established public galleries for the emerging interest in art, following the Philadelphia model with associated academies to spread passion for the arts at a grassroots level.

For his part, J. J. Haverty returned to Atlanta with the first piece of his art collection: a steel engraving of Sir Walter Scott talking to two young boys. He also left Philadelphia with a firm appreciation of the power of art as a way to uplift and bring together diverse classes of people. Throughout his life, Haverty was motivated by the simple idea, epitomized by the Centennial Exhibition, that art was essential for all Americans, rich and poor, black and white.

Haverty was a young father in Atlanta when Oscar Wilde came to the city as part of a widely acclaimed tour of the states in 1882 and 1883. A brilliant young Irish-born writer, Wilde was still in his twenties, and his most famous work—including his novel *The Picture of Dorian Gray*—was still ahead of him. The young writer thrilled the American crowds with his witty monologues and passionate pleas for support of the arts. Described by Atlanta newspapers as the "great esthete," Wilde urged listeners to appreciate the finer things in life. "Art should be generous…and seen everywhere," he said. J. J. Haverty and others in the audience nodded their heads in agreement and applauded as Wilde declared that all aspects of life were related to art and that people should "love art for its own sake and then all things that you need will be added to you."[30]

Wilde's appearance was fleeting, but it fueled further momentum for the aesthetic movement. With the economy growing again, consumers had more money, and they were more eager than ever to spend it on their homes. During the first half of the nineteenth century, plain white wall coverings and simple decorations were considered discreet and tasteful. But tastes changed in 1880s, the high-water mark for the Victorian era. Ornate decorations were vogue, exemplified by the wide popularity of ornately textured linoleum-like wall coverings known as Lincrusta-Walton. An 1885 Atlanta newspaper editorial described the overall trend:

> We are pleased to note the increasing interest manifested by our people in art matters. It is an unerring index of cultivation and refinement. We have taken moderate strides in this direction, from the simple fact that since the war we were compelled to look after the more practical duties of life in providing for its necessary wants; but now that we have passed the point that our everyday

needs are less a source of care, we will be able to take a deeper interest in everything that will tend to beautify our homes.

Following the Centennial Exhibition, civic leaders across the country quickly grasped that art museums could become powerful engines of cultural growth. The largest cities waged fierce battles to entice artists and curators and to raise capital to develop lavish marble galleries for the public. The aesthetic movement of the late nineteenth century was far bigger than sports. In this era before electronic entertainment distractions, the arts dominated the attention of the media, and cultural organizations developed at an astonishing rate.

An example of a city where the arts fueled development was Cincinnati, a critical railroad junction for anyone traveling north from Atlanta during the late 1800s. J. J. Haverty frequented the so-called Queen City along the Ohio River, which was served by the Western & Atlantic Railroad. Cincinnati around the turn of the century prided itself on its cosmopolitan flair. Prominent women in the community put their city at the forefront of the aesthetic movement and set the stage for an impressive museum that opened in 1903. Thanks to the largesse of local patrons, the city was a haven for influential American artistic talents such as sculptor Hiram Powers and painters Robert S. Duncanson, Frank Duveneck, Robert Henri, and John H. Twachtman, some of whose work would later appear on the walls of J. J. Haverty's Villa Clare.

Cotton State Exposition

Like their peers in Cincinnati, a select group of Atlantans was conscious of the need to reach out and promote Atlanta in the quest for investment and growth. Following the Civil War, a group of determined civic leaders began a quest to make Atlanta the capital of Georgia, wresting the distinction from sleepy Milledgeville in Middle Georgia, site of a major sanatorium. The effort paid off, and in 1887 construction began on the new Georgia capitol building in downtown Atlanta, not far from the Haverty & Daly Shamrock Saloon and across the street from the childhood home of Clara Malone Haverty, J. J. Haverty's wife. The gold-domed building boosted the local economy and provided a rare opportunity for artistic expression. The names of the artists recruited to carve statues for the building are no longer recorded, but they most likely encountered J. J. Haverty when they came to Atlanta. J. J.'s wife Clara posed as the model for one of the feminine figures on the Georgia state capitol tympanum, a triangular area over the building's doors on which symbolic sculptures were carved.[31]

With the capitol still under construction, a group of prominent Atlantans seized an opportunity to promote their hometown through a large public fair and at the same time charter a new social organization, the Piedmont Driving Club. Located at an old farm on the fringes of the city, the 1887 Piedmont Exposition was a cross between a state fair and an industrial exposition. Despite its modest scope, the investors had enough clout to entice President Grover Cleveland to speak, an event that drew 50,000 people. They turned a profit of nearly $10,000 for the twelve-day festival while drawing rave reviews in the national press and raising the profile of their city. The event also had the intended consequence of clearing the way for Piedmont Park, the city's first common area and a milestone in its commercial and cultural development.[32]

A few years later, Atlantans could only marvel with a touch of envy as Chicago pulled off perhaps the greatest American festival ever, the "White City" Columbian Exposition of 1893. By this time, many of Atlanta's leaders wanted a piece of the commercial prosperity and growth that seemed reserved only for cities of the North. The genius behind the "White City," Chicago's Daniel Burnham, set a new standard for how to stage a complex project for the betterment of a community. He pulled together diverse interests—public and private, artistic and commercial. All of the pieces merged in an unforgettable triumph. Atlanta did not have Burnham, but during this post-Reconstruction phase the city was home to several inspired and visionary leaders. For instance, *Atlanta Constitution* editor Henry Grady was a powerful voice in the 1870s and 1880s for change and growth. Grady was an idealist, but he knew how to coin a phrase. He articulated a clear vision of Atlanta as the capital of a progressive and tolerant new South.

Grady played a crucial role in pulling together the Piedmont Exposition of 1887, and he helped lay the groundwork for the much larger Cotton States Exposition of 1895, although he did not live to see the event. The Cotton States Exposition had financial and other problems, but it was a public relations success. One of the unsung heroes of the Cotton States Exposition was Grady's close friend, an artist named Horace Bradley. Bradley was born into Atlanta's tightly knit Irish Catholic community in 1860, two years after J. J. Haverty. The two boys went to the same church and traveled in the same circles in Civil War Atlanta. Although there is no documented correspondence between them, Haverty and Bradley had a lot in common and numerous mutual friends and acquaintances—including artist Henry O. Tanner. Bradley hired the talented African-American artist to manage his Atlanta studio for a while.[33]

Both Haverty and Bradley loved art; the difference was that Bradley had talent for creating it. In his twenties, he moved to New York, but he made a point to keep in touch with his friends in Atlanta, especially Henry Grady. Bradley was a charismatic figure and something of an Atlanta celebrity in his day, with his career adventures followed closely in the parlors of his hometown. Grady recruited him to write an "Art Talk" column for the *Atlanta Constitution* to describe the latest trends from the scene in New York. Grady also recuited Bradley as chief of the fine arts department of Atlanta's Cotton States Exposition of 1895. It was a job Bradley undertook with zeal as he traveled across America and Europe, collecting hundreds of items for display. Bradley was personally acquainted with many of the country's leading artists, including Childe Hassam, William Merritt Chase, Mary Cassatt, and Henry O. Tanner. They knew and respected Bradley as a peer. At his behest, each of these artists displayed at the Cotton States Exposition. It is no coincidence that each was later represented in Haverty's collection.

One of the big problems with staging a large fair in Atlanta was location. At the time, Atlanta was off the beaten path. While it was more accessible than Mississippi or Florida, few Americans had reason to go there or even pass through. Georgia governor W. T. Atkinson described the Southern sense of isolation at the time in an 1895 essay:

> The South remains largely an unknown land to the average Northerner, and its topography, flora and fauna, habits and customs, are almost as unfamiliar to him as to the unraveled inhabitant of another continent. Shut off from any close communication with each other for the first two-thirds of the century by vital differences in their labor systems, the Northerner first became acquainted with the real aspect of the South as a member of an invading army.[34]

Atlanta gained valuable media coverage with glowing descriptions of the Cotton States Exposition.

> Passing through the gateway the visitor will find himself within an enclosure containing a hundred and eighty nine acres of undulating surface. The spot is specially adapted for the purposes of an Exposition. In the middle is a lake covering thirteen acres, around which are grouped the various buildings arranged as far as possible to allow a water frontage. The landscape effects, including the tropical garden are exceedingly pretty, and the diversified appearance of the whole park together with the groupings of trees and shrubs, the wide avenues, the lovely tints of the foliage and the bright clear waters of the lake all combine to form a picture pleasing to the eye.[35]

Probably the best-known event from the festival was a speech by Booker T. Washington, the black educator and community leader. Washington appealed to racial harmony and denounced African-

American agitation in remarks that drew wild applause from the mostly white audience. The exposition also vaulted the young educator onto the national stage and led to strong financial support for his Tuskegee Institute, which became the premier cultural center of African Americans.

Black artists were included in the Cotton States Exposition, but they were treated shabbily. When Horace Bradley traveled to France on a mission to recruit talent for the upcoming Atlanta exposition, he made a point to pay a visit to his former tenant Henry O. Tanner. After just a few years in Paris, Tanner had made a name for himself as a premier talent. Bradley managed to coax Tanner into sending to the Atlanta show three of his best paintings, including *The Bagpipe Lesson*, a painting being sought at the time by the prestigious Pennsylvania Academy. Tanner rejected the museum's offer and instead sent his work to Atlanta. A panel of Cotton States judges awarded Tanner's painting a bronze medal, but the painting was not even exhibited along with the rest of the paintings and sculptors in the elegant fine arts building. Black artists were relegated to the Negro Pavilion because of the organizers' strict policy of segregation.

Back in his hometown after his stint in St. Louis, thirty-eight-year-old J. J. Haverty strolled through the grounds of the Cotton States Exposition, no doubt recalling his experience twenty years earlier at the Centennial Exhibition in Philadelphia. The spectacle made a particular impression on his oldest son Clarence, along with most everyone else in the city. Atlantans were intoxicated by the energy of the gathering, and there was a collective letdown once the exposition closed down at the end of the year. Across the spectrum of society, the city tried to fill the void by establishing a permanent collection of art, a place where beauty and creative energy could flourish year-round.

Bradley summed up the optimistic vision using the flowery language typical of his day: "My dream of happiness is to see in our own Atlanta a building, the very picture of architectural beauty towering like a monument among her stately structure, an edifice that would be an ornament to any people, and on it should be carved three letters, 'ART.'" If Bradley seemed a little over-enthusiastic, it was understandable. The goal of a new museum for Atlanta seemed simple and well within grasp. The new century appeared to offer tremendous promise and opportunity. But the handful of people dedicated to the arts in Atlanta could not envision the many obstacles that lay ahead in their path.

"An institution is the lengthened shadow of one man."

Ralph Waldo Emerson (a quote on the desk of J. J. Haverty)

Commerce and Beyond

After he returned to Atlanta from the Centennial Exhibition in 1876, J. J. Haverty found his job at Ryan's waiting for him. A gruff, self-made Irishman, Ryan took a liking to the hard-working young clerk. But the world of downtown Atlanta retailers was small, and the young J. J. Haverty found other opportunities. He was hired as manager for the carpet department of a newer and more upscale store, M. Rich & Bros., later Rich's. This business was run by Morris Rich, who has been described as a Hungarian Horatio Alger, a reference to his scrappy determination to succeed against tough odds. Rich was Haverty's mentor, and he understood as well as anyone the importance of reputation in late-nineteenth-century retailing. One of the company's maxims was "People are more important than things." During the lawless days after the Civil War, carpetbaggers, con artists, and snake oil salesmen preyed on vulnerable shoppers. In this climate of little or no protection for consumers, Rich operated under the novel assumption that it made good business sense to offer quality merchandise on favorable terms to the customer.

This motto of doing right by the customer was something that Haverty took to heart. In 1885, he decided it was time to go out on his own. He scraped together $600 in capital and was approved for a loan of another $600 from James English of the Lowery Bank, later the First National Bank of Atlanta. While continuing to work for Rich's, Haverty opened his own showroom downtown at 14 Hunter Street.

Building a loyal base of customers

From the beginning, family and business were closely intertwined in Haverty's life. The original partner of his furniture business was older brother Michael, the saloon keeper and Civil War veteran. When he wasn't at the bar, Michael helped to mind the store while Haverty was on duty at Rich's. And then there was Clara, J. J. Haverty's bride. Clara Malone and J. J. Haverty grew up as neighbors. Their fathers were members of the Immaculate Conception parish and each served as Fulton County tax assessor. Sometime during the late 1870s, as Clara blossomed into a beautiful woman, J. J. began the elaborate ritual of Victorian courtship, bringing flowers and gifts to the Malone residence and arranging chaperoned meetings with the daughter of his father's friend. As for the quietly confident young merchant, he cut a dashing figure with a handlebar mustache and high-collared shirt. He made his intentions perfectly clear, and in 1880 J. J. and Clara were married.

Five years later, after two children and more on the way, the couple opened Haverty Furniture Co. for business. As J. J. juggled two jobs, the industrious Clara set aside her domestic responsibilities to come to the family's tiny 25-foot-wide store at night to balance the books.

At first, business was tough. "The store had only one price: anything we could get," said J. J. Haverty. Their approach was to sell whatever furniture people wanted, and the selection was limited. "This was the Black Walnut Era, when the ten-piece bedroom set was greatly in demand. This included a Gothic bed, a bureau, a washstand with marble top, a towel rack, an uncomfortable living room rocker known as a gentleman's rocker, four straight chairs and a center table. Often the furniture was too large to be carried in doors and furniture for a second story had to be hoisted up with black and tackle."[36]

Haverty managed to distinguish his stores by adopting the customer-friendly approach he learned from Rich's. Then he added a financing twist. Since furniture was expensive and few customers could afford to buy with cash, Haverty would offer merchandise with little money down. Thus, customers were able to enjoy the furniture in their homes while paying for it later. By extending this trust, Haverty built a loyal customer base, and his business reaped the benefit of collecting interest on the payments. In addition to providing an additional and predictable stream of revenue, the easy credit policy also gave the company's commission-based salesmen the opportunity to visit customers in their homes. Driving horse-drawn buggies door to door, agents collected payments while distributing photographs offering the company's latest merchandise and deals. The face-to-face contact was essential to Haverty's early success. Others emulated it, but Haverty had a head start as a pioneer in "selling on time," and he stayed ahead of the competition by tinkering with and eventually perfecting the formula. "I am proudest of the system established early in my career, which provided every homemaker with an opportunity to obtain beautiful furniture to provide his family with more pleasant surroundings than he could otherwise afford. This was by selling furniture on the installment plan," J. J Haverty said.[37]

By 1887, the business moved to a larger location on Whitehall Street. Here, Haverty had more floor space to show furnishings, and he was able to attract more walk-in customers through all important window displays. He also had the benefit of a remarkable new invention and business development tool: the telephone. The phone number, 493, was easy to remember and was published not only in newspaper advertisements but also the city's first phone directory.

Joining forces with Rhodes

As Haverty's business grew, he attracted the attention of more-established rivals. For instance, A.G. Rhodes was a formidable Atlanta furniture retailer who had a similar program to "sell on time." They struggled head to head, and then in 1889, Rhodes proposed an alternative. He offered the younger Haverty a deal to join forces. Haverty agreed to the merger, which provided him enough stability to finally quit his job at Rich's. With the new work arrangement, Haverty was able to move his family of six out of a small apartment and into a two-story home with a veranda at 417 South Pryor Street. His growing business needed help, and J. J. Haverty invited his father, Thomas, to join the newly formed Rhodes-Haverty business as a clerk. But the old railroad laborer and saloon keeper didn't take to the indoor regimen. Thomas Haverty preferred gardening, and he soon quit. With the start of the Rhodes-Haverty partnership, Michael Haverty started his own store at 77 Whitehall, going into business with his seventeen-year-old son. But Michael lacked his younger brother's business acumen and zeal for hard work. The Michael Haverty father-son team went broke, closed up shop, and returned to the established business of Rhodes-Haverty to work as clerks.

Rhodes-Haverty was built to grow, and during the early 1890s J. J. Haverty was assigned to St. Louis. From the bustling Midwest city on the Mississippi River, he managed and opened additional stores in Missouri, Tennessee, Mississippi, and Texas. The formula for expansion was simple and effective. J. J. scouted for potential markets in his territory. From St. Louis, he boarded riverboats going up and down the Mississippi or took the railroad to most every moderately sized city within a 300-mile radius. If the conditions looked promising, he would make an offer to form a partnership with a local furniture retail concern. The deal was always the same: the local merchant would run the office and get a minority position in a new business, with Haverty and Rhodes keeping equal positions in the majority. With the local merchant as minority partners, they had an incentive to perform while Haverty and Rhodes retained control.

Looking for boomtowns

The system worked well, and Haverty established numerous contacts during his frequent travels across the nation's heartland. He understood the importance of relationships and often courted prospective business partners over drinks or by inviting them and their families to dinner. As he made his way from town to town, Haverty took careful note of the rise of the consumer class and how the economic and technological changes of the day were transforming the social and commercial landscape. He had a sharp eye for demographic conditions in an age when accurate data was scarce and big-money decisions depended on little more than gut feeling.

Haverty was fascinated by the mysterious yet powerful forces that transformed certain barren landscapes into boomtowns while other parts of the country languished. During the Victorian era, art was a common thread of conversation for educated classes, and Haverty made it a point to supplement his knowledge of this important topic. Haverty learned a lot about various markets by evaluating the relative strength of the local art community. He liked to introduce the topic of art into conversation. If there was little reaction, or if nobody cared or knew about the fine arts, then it was reasonable to assume that the community had small-minded leadership and limited potential for growth. By contrast, a vibrant local arts community was a good clue that the city was intent on growth and expansion. Haverty and other civic leaders in Atlanta frequently put forth this argument later in his career as they sought to cultivate support for the arts.

Haverty left St. Louis to return to Atlanta just before the Cotton States Exposition in 1895. Clara and the growing family were glad to return to their Pryor Street home. But then their fifth child Ben died as a baby. Shortly afterwards, J. J.'s father Thomas died, followed by Michael in 1907. Despite the personal traumas, Haverty was heavily invested in his business, and he continued his life on the road without complaint. In many ways, the turn of the century era is defined by rail travel, with the construction of cathedral-like train stations in cities across the country. Haverty took full advantage of the leap of transportation technology during his lifetime, as Atlanta was well served by the region's expanding rail network. Yet the experience of life on the rails, despite its romantic allure, could be arduous, especially for a family man such as J. J. Haverty. He spent several days a week traveling in crowded trains that made frequent stops en route to sterile hotels. This lifestyle took a toll on his personal life. But Clara and the family back in Atlanta were supported by a strong network of extended family. Moreover, as business progressed, the Haverty's lifestyle in downtown Atlanta became increasingly comfortable, with chickens, cows, and horses in the backyard and a wide porch with rocking chairs in the front.

While spending much of his life away from home, Haverty gained exposure to invaluable business contacts across the country at a pivotal time in the nation's economic expansion. He also was in a position to capitalize on historic opportunities, including the development of Texas during the early days of the great oil boom. In 1907, Haverty watched in amazement as wagonloads of families set down roots in the plains of north Texas. "I often see whole families in wagons moving from one part of the state to some other part. A number of people live in tents on account of the scarcity of homes," he wrote at the time. Not long afterward, he opened a store in Dallas, which proved to be a very lucrative market for his business.

The turn of the century was a time of rapid growth for Rhodes-Haverty, which was well positioned to take advantage of a new consumer economy that was spreading—even to the isolated cities of the Southeast. A vibrant middle class was taking root, and a spirit of optimism was spreading as prices fell and living standards rose. In Atlanta, the railroad hub of the Southeast, sidewalks teemed with well-dressed shoppers, and modern conveniences such as plumbing, electricity, and plush furniture were increasingly affordable and widespread. Life in this newly industrialized South was often frenetic and far from idyllic, especially for African Americans who were subject to oppressive Jim Crow laws or for thousands of uneducated farm hands who flocked into Atlanta to collect pitiful wages in factory jobs. But for respected business people who had access to capital, the early days of the twentieth century were highly conducive to commerce and wealth creation. Business was especially promising in the residential sector where J. J. Haverty concentrated his considerable energies. Interest rates were low, and the pace of homebuilding was intense as Atlanta's population swelled from about 90,000 in 1900 to more than 150,000 in 1910.[38]

Across Atlanta, an ambitious network of electric streetcars built by developer Joel Hurt and other real-estate titans whisked passengers to and from posh new neighborhoods such as Ansley Park, Druid Hills, and Inman Park. Inhabiting these well-appointed homes were status-conscious consumers eager to distinguish themselves through home furnishings. Ambitious merchants such as Haverty were happy to oblige.

Moving up the social ladder

With his business success, Haverty had little trouble moving up the social ladder in his hometown. Although his Catholic upbringing might have been an obstacle in certain settings, Haverty had little trouble gaining invitations to Atlanta's leading social clubs. He was invited to the Piedmont Driving Club, the Capital City Club, and the Old Guard of the Gate City Guard, the third being a group of Atlantans dedicated to reuniting the North and South and repairing the bonds of union damaged during the Civil War. Although he seemed proud of his associations as a civic leader, Haverty was not the backslapping type and did not enjoy preferred gentlemen's pastimes of hunting or sports competition. Once, he said he tried to play golf and found the experience so frustrating that he refused to swing another club. Haverty was not interested in social climbing or other superficial pursuits, and he had little use for formal parties or other stodgy rituals that distinguished the moneyed class of the day. "He has never cared to engage to any extent in conventional social life, preferring the quiet of his home," wrote Haverty's son Clarence in a description of his father's life.

As the eldest, Clarence had a unique viewpoint on J. J. Haverty's life, which he described as "a continuous series of hard won business successes."[39] Born in 1881 in a small tenement apartment and raised in his family's crowded home on Whitehall, Clarence Haverty grew into a world of private schools, servants, stables filled with beautiful horses, country clubs, and lavish ballroom parties. He was the most focused of J. J.'s children, a quiet and well-behaved boy who spent his time playing piano and reading. He watched his father closely to learn his successful habits, and after high school he carried the burden of working six days a week for the family business from 7 A.M. to 6 P.M. as his younger siblings enjoyed the privileges of newfound affluence. All of J. J.'s sons went on to work for the family business, with varying degrees of success, but Clarence was the most reliable and the obvious choice to eventually succeed J. J. Haverty.

Clarence was on his own in 1899 when the family moved again into 373 W. Peachtree Street, a sprawling two-story home with Grecian columns, a stable of horses, and a garage for the family automobile—one of the first in Atlanta. By this point in his career, J. J. Haverty was a majority partner in a business that owned a network of seventeen furniture stores, along with various other business enterprises, including a dry goods company and a novelty store.[40] He was a tough boss with a style that might be described as an iron fist in velvet glove. Writing about his father late in life, Clarence described J. J. Haverty as a "modest man who was almost timid." But he added that when it came to "active business combat," his father was fiercely competitive. He had a formal demeanor that exuded quiet authority. Once, when one of his managers was falling short, he personally sent him a lengthy note of detailed instructions on all aspects of business operations, from stock buying to advertising, to collections, and deliveries. He was not prone to shout and bang his fists on the table, but his piercing steel-blue gaze could chill the spines of friends and adversaries alike. His style was to lead by example, and on many occasions, J. J. Haverty invited favored managers into his personal office for a post-meeting chat, recalled his grandson and former Haverty's Furniture Co. Chairman and Chief Executive Rawson

Haverty. "Close the blinds," J. J. would tell his guest, while reaching for a bottle of bourbon. "It's time for a drink."

An amicable split

A pivotal time for the business was 1908. Sales were booming, and the agreement between Rhodes and Haverty was working out nicely. But the future was cloudy for Clarence, and that posed a problem for the future of the business. Rhodes also had an ambitious son who was involved with the company and angling for control as well. As an amicable way to avoid inevitable conflict, the partners devised a simple but fair way to divide the company. They flipped a coin to see who would pick first and began taking turns selecting stores, with each partner getting eight stores. Both Rhodes and J. J. Haverty wanted the downtown store at the corner of Peachtree and Auburn Avenue, and they had no agreement for splitting it until the Haverty family devised a solution to control the Atlanta market. One day, the Havertys arrived at Rhodes's office with a briefcase full of $500 bills, and J. J. and Clarence made it clear they wanted to buy the Atlanta store. With the cash resting on his desk, Rhodes paused and then dumped the neatly stacked bills into his drawer. He laughed and waved J. J. and Clarence out his office.

As rival business owners, Rhodes and Haverty kept a cordial relationship. For many years, they avoided head to head competition, although they warily eyed one another in new markets (Rhodes closed in 2005 while Havertys remains in business). The reorganized Haverty Furniture Co. was owned 50/50 with Clarence and J. J. Haverty, and further reorganization relieved the senior Haverty of much of the burden of non-stop travel. While he enjoyed spending more time with his family in Atlanta, he maintained a rigid work regimen. His unwavering routine was to wake up at 5:00 A.M. and walk briskly for an hour as a way to stay fit and clear his mind. He would then have breakfast with his wife and children before boarding the streetcar downtown to the Haverty office. "Father was a great gentleman and we all loved him, but he was pretty strict. We had to get up and get dressed to go down to breakfast," recalled Katherine, J. J.'s youngest child.[41]

Sundays were cherished days of rest for J. J. Haverty and his family. The morning was devoted to mass, and the Haverty's white-columned home on West Peachtree was only a short walk to Sacred Heart Church at the corner of Peachtree and North Pryor. During the early 1900s, the church was in debt and in need of furnishings and decoration. J. J. and Clara Haverty responded to the call from the Marist priests, who ran the parish, and along with five other families bought twenty-one stained glass windows that were installed in 1902.

At home, J. J. Haverty was an avid reader who was finding more and more time to enjoy Atlanta's limited selection of cultural events, such as opera or a lecture or perhaps a performance by a traveling theater troupe. He and his wife Clara had an active social life, and once while they were out at a formal Christmas ball at the Piedmont Driving Club, their home on West Peachtree caught fire and nearly burned to the ground. The children, who were home with a babysitter, escaped but were traumatized by the loss of their Christmas presents. Unfazed, J. J. Haverty repaired the damage, moved the family back into the house, and continued his routine. As a wealthy man in his fifties, Haverty was at a point where he could slow down this routine and begin to take it easy with life, but he was an extremely energetic man who was uncomfortable with idle pursuits. He thrived on challenges—on making a difference. As someone who had seen death in his immediate family, he understood that life was short, and he was determined to use his time remaining on Earth to full effect.

"...the liberated lower orders of whites have borrowed the worst commercial bounderism of the Yankee and superimposed it upon a culture that, at bottom, is but little removed from savagery. Georgia is at once the home of the cotton-mill sweater, of the Methodist parson turned Savanarola and of the lynching bee."

H. L. Mencken

Memorials to the Lost Cause

Given his boyhood memories of the burning of Atlanta and his brother's experience in the Confederate Army, J. J. Haverty had deep feelings about the Civil War throughout his life. And so on 11 October 1911 he joined some 75,000 people who were on hand for a Civil War reunion at Atlanta's Piedmont Park. Like the legions of graying Civil War veterans, the fifty-three-year-old J. J. Haverty wore a military uniform—not the blue or gray of the great armies of the Civil War—but the makeshift uniform of the Old Guard, the host of this occasion. This good-natured parade and picnic in Piedmont Park was dedicated to the unveiling of a new sculpture designed to commemorate the reconciliation of

North and South. Among the distinguished guests for this occasion were Georgia governor Hoke Smith and Connecticut governor Simeon Baldwin, along with Atlanta mayor C. S. Winn.

As a member of the general committee of the Old Guard, J. J. Haverty had a hand in selecting the artist for the bronze sculpture: Allen G. Newman. A former soldier, Newman was comfortable working with bronze and military themes at a time when cities across the United States were evaluated according to the size and beauty of their Civil War memorials. Newman had designed a sculpture to commemorate the Battle of Vicksburg, and his highly regarded pieces also mark historic events in Rhode Island, Pennsylvania, and elsewhere. Newman's sculpture in Piedmont Park was cast in bronze in honor of Atlanta's peace missions to the North some thirty years earlier. At the base of the sculpture, readers can find in faded bronze relief a few lines acknowledging the South's defeat and the region's willingness to "accept in good faith the result of that heroic struggle."

As a successful businessman in Atlanta, Haverty no doubt responded to the theme of peace and reconciliation represented by Newman's sculpture. Civil War reunions were common across the South around the turn of the century, and the Old Guard was involved in hosting many of these events, which had the effect of boosting local business and civic pride. The history of the Gate City Guard goes back to the earliest days of Atlanta in the 1850s, when the group formed to protect law-abiding families and to keep the peace in a railroad outpost notorious for violent crime. With the start of combat in the Civil War, many members of the Gate City Guard (including J. J.'s brother Michael Haverty) volunteered for the Confederacy and served with distinction in the Virginia theater.

After the surrender of Confederate forces and the occupation of the South, the leaders of the Gate City Guard were among the first to accept the hard reality of defeat. Instead of dwelling on the war of the past, these prominent Atlantans shifted their focus to peace of the future. The Gate City Guard was led by pragmatists in search of opportunity, not vengeance. As a result, they redefined the group around a positive message of rebuilding and strengthening ties with the more prosperous North. In 1879, the Gate City Guard led a group of Atlanta's leading citizens on a series of peace missions to the North. These events were successful in terms of public relations and may have contributed to Atlanta's economic development at a time of widespread poverty throughout the South.

Over the years, the Gate City Guard continued to evolve as the veterans began to drift away and die and a new generation assumed leadership. In 1910, the Old Guard of the Gate City Guard was formed to continue the outreach mission, and younger men such as businessman Joseph Burke and J. J Haverty, both members of the general committee, led them. The Old Guard formed during a patriotic time in the United States. North and South had recently joined forces to win the Spanish-American War and launch a new American empire overseas. They carried the flame of economic development while also vowing to preserve local history.

Debacle on Stone Mountain

With the passage of time, attitudes and depictions about the Civil War changed, and the repressed anger of the Reconstruction era began to resurface in the form of hostility to the industrial North. A new generation that had no direct experience with the horrors of combat was determined to remember their ancestors' glories—not acknowledge their defeat and reconciliation. An angrier and darker nostalgia for the Lost Cause emerged against the backdrop of the steady decline of the agrarian lifestyle represented by the old Confederacy. With the emergence of a new African-American middle class around the turn of the century, racial tensions boiled over repeatedly. Atlanta's blacks were convenient scapegoats for the economic change and continuing expansion of the industrial economy that threatened the prevailing status quo, and they endured the brunt of a violent backlash (although Catholics and Jews were also frequent targets of wrath). In 1906, vigilante mobs killed at least twelve blacks in Atlanta's African-American neighborhoods. The rioters went on a rampage when newspapers published bogus rumors about black men attacking white women.[42]

In this the era of frequent lynchings and convict labor, racism throughout Georgia intensified and the views of Robert E. Lee expanded beyond a brilliant military career; he became a mythical hero, almost godlike in his valor. In big and small cities across the old Confederacy, civic groups financed numerous memorials dedicated to the Lost Cause, creating a veritable cottage industry of sculptors and artisans. While many of these sentimental monuments proved forgettable, cities competed and invested considerable sums to build the most impressive monuments in tribute to the dwindling number of Civil War veterans.

When it came to memorials, bigger was perceived as better. And after the turn of the century, public support in Atlanta began to emerge for a carving or memorial on Stone Mountain, the world's largest granite outcropping located about 20 miles northeast of Atlanta. At 867 feet high and more than 7 miles in circumference, Stone Mountain is a fluke of geology and a marvel to behold. The Western side of the huge rock slopes gently for about a half-mile to the top, offering spectacular views of Atlanta. The northern side has a sheer face nearly a mile wide. For centuries, Indians chose Stone Mountain as a site for religious ceremonies, and more recently the landmark had been a popular destination for picnics and casual weekend hikes.

Samuel H. Venable and his family owned the property in the early 1900s, and they were eager to capitalize on this unique real estate. The land was of little use for farming. And with the emergence of the automobile and the development of paved roads, Americans were becoming increasingly mobile. Given Stone Mountain's potential as an attraction, civic leaders tossed around ideas for developing the property, and by 1915 most everyone agreed the best plan was to carve a memorial to the Lost Cause.

The Stone Mountain concept moved quickly after release of D. W. Griffith's epic silent film *Birth of a Nation*. This film's homage to white supremacy prompted a mob to burst out of the cinema and into the streets of Atlanta—yet another ugly incident in a city that was prone to racial violence. Given this tense racial climate, *Birth of a Nation* was like a spark on dry tinder. Rabblerousing segregationists such as William Simmons used the film to whip crowds into a frenzy and launch a Ku Klux Klan (KKK) for the twentieth century. Simmons revitalized the moribund racist group with a broad membership that remains a tightly guarded secret. At its peak in the mid-1920s, the KKK was known as an "invisible empire," and the group controlled hundreds of elected officials across the country. Although it was especially influential in the Midwest and claimed members as far away as Oregon, the modern KKK designated Atlanta as its headquarters, with nearby Stone Mountain as an unofficial shrine to the Lost Cause. With Simmons as leader, white supremacists inspired by *Birth of a Nation* began to flock to the summit of the granite landmark to don white hoods, burn crosses, and rant against the supposed evils of blacks, Jews, and Catholics.

Amid this racist climate, J. J. Haverty, a Catholic, publicly espoused racially inclusive and progressive views and supported one of the country's greatest African-American artists, Henry O. Tanner. Haverty also was a practical man who believed in artistic expression and economic development. He was also an admirer of history, and he saw a great deal of value in memorializing the Confederacy. From the beginning, he supported the Stone Mountain project and was glad to answer the call when his help was requested.

The initial advocates for a Stone Mountain memorial were the United Daughters of the Confederacy (UDC), led by Helen Plane. They emphasized the honor of their ancestors who fought for the Confederacy and managed to gain broad and enthusiastic support. The UDC started consulting with artists about the project, and they decided to hire renowned sculptor Gutzon Borglum.

Born in 1867 to a Mormon, Borglum was an outdoorsman who spent his youth in California and identified strongly with the mythology of the great American West. His artistic career got off to a fast start when he painted a portrait of US general John C. Fremont, nicknamed "the Pathfinder" for his adventures as a young man devising a railroad route across the rugged mountains of California. Fremont and his wife were impressed with Borglum's work and later introduced him to some of their powerful friends, including Theodore Roosevelt. Borglum honed his skills further in Europe and then opened a studio in Stamford, Connecticut. His outgoing personality and knack for self-promotion helped him gain support from some of the leading art patrons of his time. In 1907, he impressed President Theodore Roosevelt with a marble bust of Abraham Lincoln, created to commemorate the president's 100th birthday. The statue was displayed for a while in the White House and then moved to the US Capitol, where it resides today. With that notoriety, Borglum leveraged additional contacts and gained commissions for a litany of high-profile projects, including figures of the apostles at St. John the Divine in New York City and a project to redesign the torch for the Statue of Liberty.[43]

Borglum distinguished himself through the sheer size of his sculpture. His bust of Lincoln is colossal, as is his Wars of America monument in Newark, New Jersey. When Helen Plane of the UDC approached him about the Stone Mountain project, Borglum liked her idea. But he wanted to build a memorial on a larger scale. He was not interested in a sculpture that required a telescope to see. He wanted to make something that would impress people when viewed from any distance. With his dramatic flair, he described a plan to carve on the mountain an entire Confederate army, with Robert E. Lee and other generals on horseback leading columns of soldiers and cannons. He envisioned an entire "Lost Cause" theme park with an amphitheater and various family attractions. His pitch enthralled nearly everyone who heard it, and within a short time Borglum was hired to lead the biggest sculpture project in history.

As part of the deal, the Venable family agreed to turn over the property to the Stone Mountain Memorial Association, a group of leading citizens chartered to head the project. But there was a catch: the memorial would revert back to the Venable family after twelve years. In 1916 during the initial phase of the project, the deadline did not seem problematic, but it would later become the source of a bitter dispute that would frustrate J. J. Haverty and the other leaders of the project. Work was delayed during World War I, giving Borglum time to go to Washington to lobby for financial support. He helped persuade Congress to fund the memorial by minting a half-dollar coin to sell to the Stone Mountain Memorial Association. In turn, the association planned to sell the coins for a dollar each to collectors and various supporters of the project. Senator Henry Cabot Lodge of Massachusetts and Reed Smoot of Utah sponsored the plan, which called for minting 5 million coins.

President Calvin Coolidge signed the bill, and in 1923 with the economy recovering from its post-war doldrums, the first drill bit into Stone Mountain's granite. Ironically, four black laborers first installed the steel beams on the face of the mountain to support the wood platforms that would be used to carve a likeness of General Robert E. Lee. For months, the men blasted away at the face of the rock with dynamite and jackhammers. By 19 January 1924, Lee's birthday, they were ready for an unveiling of sorts: the general's giant head was complete. Borglum threw a big party, including the press and thousands of onlookers. The artists invited a few VIPs to kick off the festivities with a blustery breakfast while seated at a table perched on the face of the mountain atop Lee's unfinished shoulder.[44]

But, just as Gettysburg was for the Confederacy, Lee's birthday would prove to be the high water for the memorial project. As funding problems mounted, Borglum and the Stone Mountain Memorial Association began to clash. The association complained that Borglum was spending too much time on promotion of the project and not enough on the actual design and carving. They also wanted him to scale back the memorial to save money, a notion that did not sit well with the cantankerous artist. Borglum in turn accused association president Hollins Randolph of diverting donated funds for personal use and of running up exorbitant expense accounts.

On 25 February 1924, with work on the huge likeness of General Stonewall Jackson under way, the association fired Borglum. Enraged, the artist destroyed the model, which was a crucial reference for the memorial. The project could not continue without it. Borglum did not waste time getting out of Georgia and escaping the wrath of the association. He jumped into his car, and in one of the most unlikely high-speed chases in Georgia history, he raced across the state line, foiling the local police who were in hot pursuit. The Stone

Mountain Memorial Association charged him with malicious mischief and filed against him a $50,000 civil suit. Borglum and Stone Mountain had parted company, and this divorce freed the artist to pursue an even more ambitious project in South Dakota: Mount Rushmore.[45]

With the artist a fugitive and the project in disarray, Haverty stepped into the fray in an effort to salvage the Stone Mountain memorial. He approached Washington collector Duncan Phillips and other contacts across the nation in the art community for a recommendation of a replacement artist. The Stone Mountain project was nationally known and offered a chance for tremendous visibility. Haverty was especially impressed with Augustus Lukeman, who had completed a highly regarded bronze likeness of Ulysses Grant. Lukeman had competed with Borglum for other notable commissions of historical figures. But unlike his more volatile rival, Lukeman had a reputation as a soft-spoken professional, and this even-keel temperament was a strong selling point with the leadership of the Stone Mountain Memorial Association.

With Haverty's recommendation, the association hired Lukeman to replace Borglum, and the new artist decided to start the memorial from scratch. Lukeman blasted away Borglum's huge carvings of Lee and Jackson, and his team set about working on two new heads located below where his predecessor had begun his carvings. The project was back on track, but the original sponsors were not pleased. The competing memorial projects had made a mess of the mountainside, and by 1928 the original twelve-year deadline for completing the project was looming. On one side were the Venables, who continued to correspond with Borglum and were said to share similar sympathies for the KKK. Moreover, despite Haverty's well-documented endorsement, Lukeman was Jewish, and his ancestry did not endear him to the white supremacist Venables who owned the mountain. When it came time to renew the original agreement to build the memorial, the Venables resisted firmly. They would extend the lease for the project only on the condition that the association rehired Borglum to share leadership of the project with Lukeman. For the association, the idea of bringing back their nemesis was too much to bear.

Association leader G. H. Willis then called on J. J. Haverty as chairman of a special reconciliation committee tasked with coming to some agreement with the Venables to continue the project. Haverty used all of his diplomatic skills to keep the project on track. He tried for months to negotiate an agreement with the Venables on behalf of the association, but both sides broke off talks in September. Under no conditions would the association have anything to do with Borglum, and the Venables were not about to compromise. The original twelve-year deadline to build the memorial expired without any extension to continue the work. The mountain reverted back to the Venables, and for all practical purposes the memorial was dead—at least until the state of Georgia bought Stone Mountain in 1958 for use as a public park.

The state helped enable a redesigned Confederate memorial that was finished in 1970, some forty-five years after Gutzon Borglum fled Georgia and nearly thirty years after the death of J. J. Haverty. During those decades, the sheer face of Stone Mountain facing the north was a silent and unsightly testament to the age of nostalgia for the Lost Cause. But the modest peace sculpture by Allen Newman in Piedmont Park—now overlooked by countless joggers and pedestrians—was completed by Haverty's Old Guard during his lifetime with subsequent little fuss and fanfare. This memorial remains in place as a statement of friendship and optimism for the future.

"Art, the love of it, the appreciation of it,
the collection of it, is a pleasure and should engage the
attention of every member of society for its cultural
influence, its power of education."

J. J. Haverty, 1927

A Southern Art Collector

During the second decade of the twentieth century, Atlanta was sprawling rapidly from the crowded neighborhoods downtown toward the north along Peachtree Street. At Peachtree and Collier Road (the present location of Piedmont Hospital), Colonel Jack Spalding, founder of the law firm King & Spalding, bought a large home named Deerland. He raved about this location to his friend J. J. Haverty and pointed out that an adjacent undeveloped 6-acre parcel to the north was undeveloped and available. Haverty visited the site and liked what he saw: rolling woodlands fronting Peachtree Street and backing up to a railroad line, nestled along a steep slope of rocks and crevices where half a century earlier Union and Confederate forces fought hand-to-hand with bayonets at the Battle of Peachtree Creek. This property was not only accessible to key points of the city by streetcar, it was also a short drive to most anywhere in Atlanta—in short, a piece of land that was obviously going to increase in value. When presented with a good deal, Haverty was not one to hesitate. He bought the land and then hired architect Edward Daugherty to begin construction of his dream home. The result was a sprawling Italian-style home that he named Villa Clare, after his wife and his father's homeland of County Clare, Ireland.

Villa Clare was finished in 1916, and that year the family celebrated its first Christmas there. This new home had the latest amenities: vented kitchen appliances, copper plumbing fixtures with running water in each bathroom and—most impressively—electrical outlets and light switches in every room. Downstairs, the walls were ideal for entertaining and art, and J. J. Haverty's private office was wood paneled and packed with books. For Haverty's youngest children these were happy days; teenagers Dorothy and Katherine were delighted to explore their new home and property. But for J. J. Haverty, 1917 was a tough year. His beloved wife Clara grew increasingly ill from a debilitating kidney illness known as Bright's Disease. Moreover, Haverty's executive office was thrown into disarray in 1917 after Woodrow Wilson began to mobilize a huge military force to fight Germany. Several of J. J.'s sons who held key positions in his business and other top managers volunteered for military service. Even thirty-six-year-old Clarence—a new father and the heart and soul of his operations team—excused himself from work to begin drilling for the fight in Europe (although he never enlisted). The management of the far-flung network of furniture stores was very demanding and with his wife dying, the fifty-nine-year-old J. J. Haverty was forced to put in extra time at the Haverty's office and in the field to fill the management gap.

'A Severe Blow'

Clara's battle with Bright's Disease ended in 1918, and she was buried at Atlanta's Westview Cemetery. "My mother was an invalid during the last eight years of her life, and her death in August 1918 was a severe blow to my father," Clarence Haverty wrote. "Her gentle wonderful life was the greatest inspiration and has been the guiding spirit of her children always."[46] Soon after Clara's death, Haverty began experiencing breathing problems. He left Atlanta for an extended time to go to New Orleans for surgery at Tulane Hospital. Daughter May moved to New Orleans to care for her father, and the youngest daughters were sent to boarding school to finish their high school education. Only two years after its completion, Villa Clare stood empty.

After several months in convalescence, Haverty recovered. Through much of the ordeal of Clara's death and Haverty's subsequent illness, his oldest daughter May was there to help her father. Her brother Clarence described May as her father's "special favorite," adding that she earned this affection by her "unselfish devotion" to their father.[46] She was an attractive young woman who in her youth attracted a number of boyfriends, but she never married. After the death of her mother, she assumed the role of caretaker for her father, reading by his side and arranging for friends and priests to visit and pray during his recovery.

Haverty turned to his Catholic faith for consolation and strength to recover from this mysterious illness that disabled him following Clara's death. By the time he came back to Villa Clare, the war was over and the troops were home from France. With their return, Atlanta became a different place, less provincial and more astute. Many well-educated men from the city's finest families served in the huge expeditionary force that went to Europe. Those who survived the ordeal came home confident and worldly, ready to make their mark in the world. America's new generation of war heroes brought home a newfound taste for wine and European culture, especially art. Once they had settled down, they worked hard and married into positions of influence, raising the bar of sophistication wherever they went. The post-World War I generation blended new and old money, and they embraced new ideas and cultures. After the war, a growing number of Atlantans enjoyed an elegant lifestyle that involved frequent travel to Europe aboard lavish ocean liners. They were at ease mingling with the social elite of New York, Paris, and

London. The top of the social ladder was becoming increasingly crowded and diverse. For a growing segment of society, art was a frequent topic of conversation and a way to distinguish oneself from the uncultivated crowds.

Living in a Spirit of Jazz

With the return of American forces from Europe, a modern consumer economy began to take root and permanently reshaped life in Atlanta and America at large. This was the era of speakeasies, bathtub gin (Prohibition was the law of the land), and easy-money wheeling and dealing. It was also an era of extremes of wealth and poverty. On one hand, because of agricultural overproduction and the boll weevil, the state's agricultural economy collapsed. With countless farms insolvent, rural families flocked to Atlanta in search of work. Labor was needed for textile mills and other factories, as well as for the city's booming construction sector. Atlanta's new airport was being built, along with a system of viaducts to keep trains rolling through downtown Atlanta. "The 1920s were years of despair, reflected in part by their desperate frivolity, but in that despair lay for Georgia a cultural awakening."[48]

In Atlanta, commuters no longer required a network of electric rail cars to get around the city. With more efficient manufacturing, middle-class families could afford reliable automobile transportation. The landscape of the entire city began to change as the automobile opened access to thousands of wooded acres beyond downtown. Villa Clare on Peachtree Street was no longer on the fringe of Atlanta; it was now at the gateway to Buckhead, the new neighborhood of choice for elite families and the site of many lavish homes. During the 1920s, some of the strict social mores that constrained society during the Victorian era began to ease. And J. J. Haverty had mixed feelings about what was described at the time as an age of growing decadence. "Americans are living in a spirit of Jazz perhaps, but that doesn't mean that they lack ideals. We have weak people in every age, every generation, but they do not sway the character of the big majority, nor do they dim the beauties of the artist, the ideals of the scholar or the refinement of the average citizen," he wrote in 1925.[49]

Haverty took full advantage of the prosperity of the Jazz age. During the 1920s, Atlanta started to take on a certain swagger for the first time since Sherman burned the city. Atlantans took collective pride as native son Bobby Jones racked up golfing championships, and Coca-Cola set the standard for global marketing. It was during the 1920s that Atlanta emerged as a sprawling metropolis of paved roads and automobiles, with many of the familiar attributes of twentieth-century life. "It was a time of train stations, downtown department stores and movie palaces, swank apartment houses and smart social clubs."[50]

The early 1920s were also years of transition for J. J. Haverty. With the walls of his new home in need of decoration, he began collecting art, pursuing the acquisition of fine paintings and sculptures with characteristic zeal and energy. "My father's interests outside of his business are the pursuits of a student," wrote his eldest son Clarence. "He is a lover of art, and owns one of the most complete private collections in the South. He is not simply a collector of paintings, he is a thorough connoisseur of art. He is a student of the theatre in its best phrases and is thoroughly versed in literature, economics and current information. Such hobbies he has he rides hard, as he does everything he comes in contact with."[51]

'The gallery is his only thought'

To describe the thrill he derived from collecting art, Haverty quoted Irish art critic George A More, who said,

> I know of no more intense passion, and I will add, no more beautiful passion, than the passion for the collecting of works of art. Of all passions it is the purest; it matters little to the man possessed of it whether he collects for the state or for himself. The

> gallery is his child and all his time and energy are given to the enrichment and service of his gallery. The gallery is his only thought; he will lie awake at night to better think out his plans for the capture of some treasure on which he has set his heart. He will get up in the middle of the night and walk about the gallery, considering some project for improved arrangements.[52]

While he responded to the aesthetics of art, Haverty was a tough negotiator who recognized the intrinsic value of paintings. "To buy paintings wisely is a good business investment," he said.[53] Unlike the better-known and wealthier robber barons who hired professional collectors in their quest to appear sophisticated and worldly, Haverty did his own research. He became a voracious reader of art publications, which, due to the popularity of art and the spread of mass media during the 1920s, became available across the country. At Villa Clare, Haverty and his eldest daughter May assembled an extensive library of art books, which were later donated to the High Museum. As he became involved in art collecting, J. J. Haverty began to cultivate relationships with leading art patrons, including the noted Washington-based art critic and collector Duncan Phillips. Haverty exchanged several letters with Phillips and expressed particular admiration for his book *Art and Understanding*, along with his essays about J. Alden Weir and Arthur B. Davies.

Given his penchant for American artists, Haverty purchased most of his work from US galleries, but in 1925—an especially active year for Haverty—he traveled to London and purchased a portrait by Thomas Gainsborough of his wife and a painting entitled *Madame Schinderlin* by Joshua Reynolds (Reynolds and Gainsborough were rivals in eighteenth-century London as two of the best painters of their day, and Haverty later displayed the paintings as a pair). Records show that Haverty spent some $4,500 on paintings during his 1925 European trip (he also met Pope Pius XI in Rome and gave the pontiff a bag filled with Stone Mountain Confederate Memorial half-dollars). During 1924 and 1925, Haverty was especially aggressive in purchasing art, and he recorded twenty-two checks for paintings amounting to $25,000—about the equivalent of $282,000 in 2005 dollars.

During numerous visits to New York, Haverty negotiated directly with artists for portraits, such as a matching pair of portraits of Clara and J. J. Haverty by Charles Naegele. These works hung in his Villa Clare dining room. Other art galleries he patronized included Ferargil Gallery ($1,250 for *Path of Gold* by Jonas Lie, one of Haverty's favorite artists), Macbeth Gallery ($2,000 for *The Return of the Fishing Party* by J. Alden Weir), and Newhouse Galleries ($350 for *Mrs. Dwyer*, a drawing by John Singer Sargent). At an auction held by the American Art Galleries of New York, he bought *Sheer Light* by John Noble for $850 and John Twachtman's *Along the River* for the same price. Haverty's preferred source for acquisitions was the Grand Central Art Galleries, which represented many of the artists in the Villa Clare collection. The Grand Central Galleries was headed by Walter L. Clark, a former engineer from Philadelphia who founded the gallery along with the great American painter John Singer Sargent. Clark, a major booster of art in Atlanta, was later described by Haverty as "a man with the soul of an artist and the strength of a business genius."[54]

The Grand Central Exhibitions

Haverty's relationship with the Grand Central Galleries turned out to be a crucial catalyst in Atlanta's long quest to establish a permanent museum of the arts. The manager of the Grand Central galleries and J. J. Haverty's chief artistic consultant was Erwin Barrie. Under Barrie's management, the Grand Central Galleries prospered for much of the mid-twentieth century. Born in Canton, Ohio, Barrie attended the Chicago Art Institute and began his career as manager of a gallery at the Chicago department store Carson Pirie Scott. He was an amateur painter as well as an avid golfer; in his spare time, he enjoyed painting scenes of famous golf holes, from Augusta National to St. Andrews. Operating during this heyday of American style and class,

Barrie was a clothes horse who was known for startling customers or fellow members of the Greenwich Country Club by wearing rainbow-colored shirts, dapper hats, and other eccentric garb.[55]

The Grand Central Galleries had an egalitarian philosophy of art that appealed to Haverty, and the basic message was that no respectable home was complete without some sort of original art collection. "When the body is warmed and fed we crave beauty, which is art," wrote Walter Clark, president of the Grand Central galleries, in a brochure for the 1925 Atlanta show.

> Appreciation of art in the country is growing rapidly. It is becoming one of the great interests of the cultured part of our community. Art patrons are multiplying, art museums are being built and projected all over the country. More and more people are coming to realize that beauty is an essential of happiness. That a beautiful work of art in the home will bring happiness is a simple fact and a highly important one. The Grant Central Art Galleries were founded to help carry the message to the American people and there is no city in the country that is doing more than Atlanta to help us put forward this great work.[56]

The idea of showcasing the best of American art in Atlanta had tremendous appeal to J. J. Haverty. But traveling art exhibitions were expensive and risky; if the art did not sell, the promoter was likely to incur a loss. Galleries would not move to a city without a firm commitment of local support. Depending on the amount of money pledged up front, gallery owners needed to sell most if not all of the work to justify insurance, security, and transportation costs. Another way to build support was through the sale of membership. The Grand Central galleries had "lay members" from Los Angeles to Miami to Baltimore, and in 1923 when J. J. Haverty paid $600 for his membership, the list of cities included Atlanta.[57] Other dues-paying Atlantans included J. Carroll Payne, Samuel Inman, and Thomas Hinman.[58] No doubt this support from leaders in the community was a factor in the selection of Atlanta as a destination for the galleries' initial 1924 exhibition.

Haverty was typical of a new breed of business and civic leaders who recognized that commercial success was inadequate for a vibrant city and that arts and culture could support future growth and prosperity. "We are a vigorous city in industry, in the things that make for material greatness, in the personal ability of our public men, and in the enterprise of our citizens," Haverty wrote.[59] Because of his collection and his passion for art, he was the natural choice to lead Atlanta's artistic community, and in the 1920s he became active in the moribund Atlanta Art Association in 1923, a group founded in 1905 with a charter to "promote interest in the fine and applied arts, to give lectures and practical instruction, and to found a museum and an art school."[60] One of his first moves was to form an art committee of the Atlanta Chamber of Commerce. "Our business men must contribute to the cultural development of our people and support the many exhibitions of art which may be held here and throughout this American land," he wrote. "These exhibitions are outstanding in their cultural influence, demonstrating the fact that while leading in material prosperity and industrial institutions, we have not overlooked the cultural interests of our citizens."[61]

"Another Realm of Culture"

Haverty recognized the importance of public relations and worked hard to sell his message in the media. He courted reporters such as Helen Knox Spain, and he gained further notoriety by pledging $150,000 for a museum, provided the city would match that amount. Soon the local media began echoing his messages almost word for word. On 1 May 1925, the *Atlanta Journal* published,

> Suppose that during these last fifteen years we had had no annual spring season of opera and no autumn and winter concerts. How incomparably poorer the city would be in life and character and

> renown. Well, we are losing just that much in another realm of culture as long as we delay the establishment of an art museum. We are on the eve of our second annual exhibition of paintings and sculpture from the Grand Central Galleries, an event which thousands of Atlantans remember with keenest pleasure and to which they look forward with enthusiasm. There could be no more congenial atmosphere for the idea of a community art museum.[62]

A few days later, the *Atlanta Constitution* offered an even more glowing report:

> The announced determination of the Art Committee of the Atlanta Chamber and of the Atlanta Art Association to begin building an art museum for the city during the current year is one which cannot be too highly praised. The rapid awakening of the consciousness of the beautiful among the rank and file of Atlantans is in fact one of the most remarkable facts in civic life today. The exhibition held here last May by the Grand Central Art Galleries was probably the largest single factor in the renaissance.[63]

Haverty tried to set an example by opening his wallet to buy art, and newspapers breathlessly noted his purchases. The *Constitution* reported when during the 1924 exhibition Haverty bought two canvases by Norwegian Jonas Lie. The following year, Haverty spent another $8,500 for a large batch of paintings from the Grand Central Art Galleries, including a canvas by American figure painter Charles Hawthorne. In 1925, Haverty also bought a John Singer Sargent painting from the Macbeth Gallery, and in the fall he made a trip to France, where he spent $6,500 on art.

Others in Atlanta followed suit, purchasing some $40,000 in paintings during the 1924 Grand Central Exhibition. The total attendance was 25,000, and Haverty was pleased with the results.

"The value of these gems by recognized artists will be enhanced with the years, and they will be a daily inspiration to all who behold them, a leaven in the development of the South's artistic side. Thus, both the intrinsic value of paintings left in Atlanta and the untold cultural value of this exhibit was significant."[64]

Immediately after the 1924 show, Haverty set his sights on staging a much bigger exhibition of art for the next year, pledging ever broader community support. He persuaded Barrie to provide a much larger selection of the best American paintings from New York, and in May 1925, a southbound locomotive pulled into Atlanta's Brookwood Station. The train's cargo included hundreds of crates containing art insured for $1.25 million¸ a fortune in this pre-inflationary time. Altogether, Grand Central Galleries sent some 400 paintings and sculptures to Atlanta for an exhibition at the brand new Biltmore hotel, the largest and most elegant building between Miami and Washington, DC.[65] On display were paintings by John Singer Sargent, Impressionist Mary Cassatt, and Ernest Lawson, the third a leader of the so-called ash can school of New York artists who distinguished themselves with raw depictions of bridges and alley ways.

In Atlanta, which had a population of about 200,000, there was a wave of excitement following the success of previous year's exhibition. "Atlanta has entered upon a week to be marked by the beginning of an artistic and spiritual experience that has rarely been given another American city," noted a writer for the *Atlanta Constitution*, a sample of the typically breathless press coverage describing the event.[66]

Atlanta's second Grand Central Galleries show opened on 10 May 1925, and it was the preeminent social occasion of an era that set the standard for class and elegance. Spotlights shimmered off the front of the Biltmore's facade, and beams pierced the evening sky. A long line of cars drove under the hotel portico as uniformed valets opened doors. White-gloved ladies, draped in glittering gowns colored in springtime pastels, stepped out and strolled arm in arm with tuxedoed escorts, making their way across a red carpet and through the Biltmore's black and gold marble lobby. More than 400 of Atlanta's leading citizens, including the governor of Georgia and the mayor, arrived at the Biltmore that night, and the entertainment included a violin performance from a beautiful virtuoso along with food prepared by a French chef who had served European royalty.

At a time when there was little if any competition in the way of sports, entertainment or cultural events, the Grand Central Exhibition was a blockbuster, drawing more attention than even a much-heralded performance of the Metropolitan Opera. Over the next two weeks, more than 50,000 attended—the equivalent of one in four Atlantans. A cross-section of people lined up outside the Biltmore for hours for a chance to file through the crowded hotel and glimpse the art. Haverty was especially pleased by the diverse turnout. "It was a democratic attendance and not a high-brow affair," he said. "The great and lowly came to see and admire. The cultured and the unlettered paid homage to art. The old and young were there—the practical and the dreamers came; the old to admire and the young to drink and absorb from the fountains of beauty. The grown people were entertained and the young instructed."

The 1925 exhibition was a triumph for J. J. Haverty and the entire city of Atlanta. In a less than a handful of years, the Atlanta Art Association had demonstrated a burst of remarkable progress. National publications lauded the sales and attendance at the Grand Central Exhibitions at the Biltmore, and Haverty took justifiable pride in the moment. "The Exhibition put new life into our Art Association," he told the *American Magazine of Art*.[67] "We have increased our membership by a considerable number. We are talking and planning for a Museum of Fine Arts, and we expect to effect our plans and begin work in a short time." Through a pair of successful exhibitions, J. J. Haverty and a handful of his friends had dragged Atlanta into the twentieth century. "All at once, like a bolt of lightning from a clean sky, a few forward looking citizens of our city gathered together and brought the first great exhibition of art to Atlanta from the Grand Central Galleries of New York," Haverty said. "This exhibition opened the eyes of all Atlanta and directed the attention of its citizens to the actual meaning of art."[68]

While he clearly took satisfaction in the progress, Haverty also recognized that more work was needed. At the end of 1925, there was still no permanent museum in Atlanta—a shortcoming that Haverty would address with considerable energy in the weeks and months ahead.

Art is today a living, breathing thing in Atlanta, and its influence is becoming widespread because our people are not content to do things in a small way.

J. J. Haverty, 1927

Birth of the High Museum

Atlanta was slow to build a permanent museum, despite the best efforts of a handful of dedicated souls involved with the Atlanta Art Association. From its start in 1905, the organization was long on enthusiasm and idealism and short on clout and management acumen. The members consisted mostly of high-minded women who met informally over tea and finger food in the high-ceilinged parlors of Atlanta's finest homes while engaging in earnest discussions of primarily art, but also opera, women's suffrage and other issues of the day. They established a small downtown tearoom called the Blue Teapot to raise money and named as their first president Mrs. Nannie C. Boyd, a Nashville belle who opened the doors of her family's Peachtree Street mansion to innumerable lavish parties. During this age of formality and social hierarchy, she and her husband were frequent hosts for lectures, musical concerts, and other cultural events. Boyd was something of an ambassador for Atlanta's art scene, and she built relationships with cultural leaders in places such as St. Louis, where she was selected to serve on the fine arts awards jury of the 1904 Louisiana Purchase Exposition.[69]

The next year, Nannie Boyd collaborated with the Nashville Art Club to secure the loan of a two-week art exhibition in Atlanta that encompassed 163 paintings, including work by several artists who would later appear in the Haverty collection. The exhibition, which took place at 38 Whitehall, was marked by a lavish opening night on 29 November 1905. The aim was to support an art school for Atlanta in the mode of the Pennsylvania Academy, the learning institution that had done so much to make Philadelphia a center for art in America and drive growth in that city. Atlanta's first art school opened in 1907 with a teacher recruited from Chicago. The school offered a way for young Atlanta women to study drawing and other artistic techniques without having to relocate to New York or elsewhere.

But the school's management was as ineffectual as its timing. Not long after the school's doors opened, a series of bank panics shocked commerce across the country, and financial support evaporated. Atlanta's first art school closed in 1909, leaving the Atlanta Art Association membership disillusioned and the organization in debt. A handful of determined members tried to keep the flame of art alive informally during the days before World War I, but the fire was nearly extinguished. Mrs. Samuel M. Inman, who followed Mrs. Boyd as the association's president, recalled these uncertain times in 1909: "From that point on, we did not undertake any large project. We continued to have exhibitions and lectures, giving prizes to the public schools for improvement in gardens and the physical appearance of the school buildings; trying to arouse the people of Atlanta to the need of art in the life of a city."[70]

Art was a tough sell in Atlanta during the early twentieth century for various reasons. In addition to virulent anti-black hostility, conservatively religious norms were also suffocating. In an outburst of Puritanism, powerful preachers railed from the pulpit against immoral storefront displays, advertising, or other public expressions that did not meet their strict standards of approval. In this climate of narrow-mindedness, studying the nude form or portraying other "immoral" images was strictly off-limits. Despite flickering support from the Atlanta Art Association, people who were creatively inclined typically practiced their discipline in secret, gave up, or moved away. Then there was the problem of money. At a pre-income tax time when robber barons were pouring their fortunes into artistic institutions elsewhere, Atlanta lacked deep-pocketed patrons who were committed to developing the city's creative endeavors. Before 1920, J. J. Haverty was occupied running his business and unable to provide leadership. Scarce philanthropist dollars in the capital-starved community did not typically go toward the arts, widely considered a frill and perhaps even a sin. Writing in his essay "The Sahara of the Bozart," Baltimore columnist H. L. Mencken described the South as a "cultural desert" characterized by tastes that were "crass, gross, vulgar, and obnoxious," and he singled out Georgia as perhaps the most backward of Southern states.[71] While most everyone in Atlanta bristled, they were not in a position to retaliate. When it came to institutions of culture and the arts, Atlanta—along with most every other Southern city—paled in comparison to counterparts in other regions of the United States, a point that J. J. Haverty expressed in the 1920s as he sought to gain public support for the arts: "The cities of New York, Chicago, Cleveland, Detroit, Philadelphia, San Francisco, Los Angeles, Kansas City, Toledo and a number of other great cities of America, some no larger and some no richer than Atlanta, have institutions of art, some endowed by private citizens and some supported and maintained by public funds." [72]

A New Approach for the Arts

Support for the arts increased in the early 1920s after the mayor created the Atlanta Art Commission with Haverty as chair. This commission supported the Art Association, then led by Haverty's friend and local attorney J. Carroll Payne. Along with organizational skills, Haverty and Payne brought credibility and energy. The two men worked well together during a critical period during the mid-1920s. When Payne assumed leadership of the art association, Haverty was glad to take a back seat as vice president and then chairman while working in his preferred manner: behind the scenes. He started an art committee of the Atlanta Chamber of Commerce and proceeded to raise awareness about the arts in the business community. His approach to get a museum for Atlanta was not merely build it and they will come. Instead, Haverty figured the art should come first, that the people needed to have an understanding and appreciation of art before they would support a successful museum. "Art, the love of it, the appreciation of it, the collection of it, is a pleasure and should engage the attention of every member of society for its cultural influences, its power of education," he said.[73] His strategy was to bring the best possible art to Atlanta and encourage people to purchase it for their homes. Sooner or later, the best pieces would end up in a museum. The Grand Central Exhibitions were a key tactical success, but did not represent total victory: a permanent and thriving museum for Atlanta.

Among the honored guests who attended the 1925 Grand Central Exhibition was Mrs. Joseph Madison "Hattie" High, a widow whose late husband was the owner of a successful Atlanta department store chain. J. J. Haverty described High as a "splendid and public-spirited woman." An enthusiastic daughter of the American Revolution and the Confederacy,[74] she was not actively involved in the city's art community but was well aware of the travails experienced by local museum advocates. Haverty was a friend and business associate of her late husband. Haverty carefully planted the idea that sponsorship of a new museum would be a fitting tribute to the late Mr. High, and Haverty made sure Mr. High's widow was given royal treatment at the Grand Central Exhibitions. She was particularly impressed by the outpouring of support for the 1925 show and by a subsequent essay Haverty published titled "Art and Its Meaning." The article appeared in the *Atlanta Constitution* and expressed his vision for an institution of the arts. In May 1926, after several more months of behind-the-scenes discussion with Haverty and other leaders of the Art Association, High made a stunning announcement. She had agreed to donate her home at 1262 Peachtree to the Atlanta Art

Association "to be used as a permanent museum of art for the city of Atlanta." According to High's instructions, the property also was to include an art school. The museum was intended as a permanent memorial for her late husband and was to be named the High Museum of Art. The presentation, she told a reporter, "was something of which I had been thinking a long time.... I saw the need of an art museum in Atlanta, and I recognized the great desire of the city's art lovers for such an institution."[75]

The third annual Grand Central Exhibition took place in October 1926 at Atlanta's new museum, High's home. The original High house was built in Tudor style in 1911, and it offered spacious halls and twenty rooms, ideal for an exhibition. Situated north of downtown in what was then a residential district near Ansley Park and about 2 miles south of Villa Clare, the museum offered 27,000 square feet—more than twice the space of the New Orleans museum and bigger than Nashville's Parthenon replica. The donation of Mrs. High's home was matched by a gift of $12,400 from Lucius Perry Hills, funds which formed the nucleus of a building fund. With these donations, Atlanta took a huge step toward its goal of being the leading cultural destination in the South. The new High Museum and Art School were dedicated in fall 1926 with effusive accolades for the lady who offered her home as a museum for the people of Atlanta.

While the pledge from Mrs. High was a milestone and a breakthrough, the Atlanta Art Association members were acutely aware that a functioning museum required more than brick and mortar. Under Haverty's leadership, the association petitioned the Fulton County and Atlanta governments to support the infant museum, arguing that an institution of the arts would boost the local economy. "Atlanta is far behind other cities of the South of the same class in providing for art education and training. The necessity of an art museum is quite as important as a library or as public schools [sic]. All of these are part of the city's educational facilities and are so recognized by all the great cities in America," they argued.[76]

Although local officials were not persuaded to offer public funds for the museum, efforts to rally private support for the arts were successful. Haverty launched the Friends of the Arts fund as a way to syndicate contributions to the High Museum, ranging from $5 to $5,000. Anyone who contributed $500 was in the Founders Class, $1,000 earned people Patrons Class, and the twelve members who donated $5,000 qualified for Life Class. Haverty and a handful of others rallied support through relentless solicitation and the distribution of dissertations about the power of the arts. In a letter asking for money for the new museum, Payne, then president of the association, wrote in 1928, "In most of us there is an inarticulate, undefined longing for the beautiful things of this world. When this is properly directed it will flood the lives of the people with light and color, widening their narrow confines and making life richer, fuller and more satisfying."[77]

The syndication program attracted support from well-known families, including Edward and Emily Inman, Mildred Inman High, Hugh and Josephine Richardson, John and Sara Slaton, Henry and Roberta Inman, and Frank and Louise Inman.[78] The proceeds were used to form the nucleus of a permanent collection, including paintings by English painter Joshua Reynolds and Italian painter Giambattista Tiepolo. In the final years of the go-go 1920s, the High Museum made rapid progress, with the help of the Atlanta Art Association's various presidents: Haverty and Payne, Frank Lowenstein of Norris, Inc., and then Coca-Cola's Harrison Jones. Mrs. High donated an auditorium in 1929, and Walter Hill, president of the Retail Credit Corporation, provided financial support. Another top priority was to hire a director, and Haverty took the lead in this recruitment effort. During the 1920s, experienced museum directors were scarce, and the position commanded top dollar, given the broad interest in art across the country and the addition of numerous museums. Haverty asked Lawrence Coleman of the Smithsonian Institution for help in finding a qualified candidate, offering $200 a month for a position in "charge of the museum and its activities." He added, "Our little museum is starting off well. We have about 30 or 40 paintings of our own and several good loans. We have about 40 pupils in our art classes. We have had a number of 'one man' and other exhibitions since the museum opened last October."[79] By 1928, the High Museum had 1,000 members, an endowment of $100,000 and

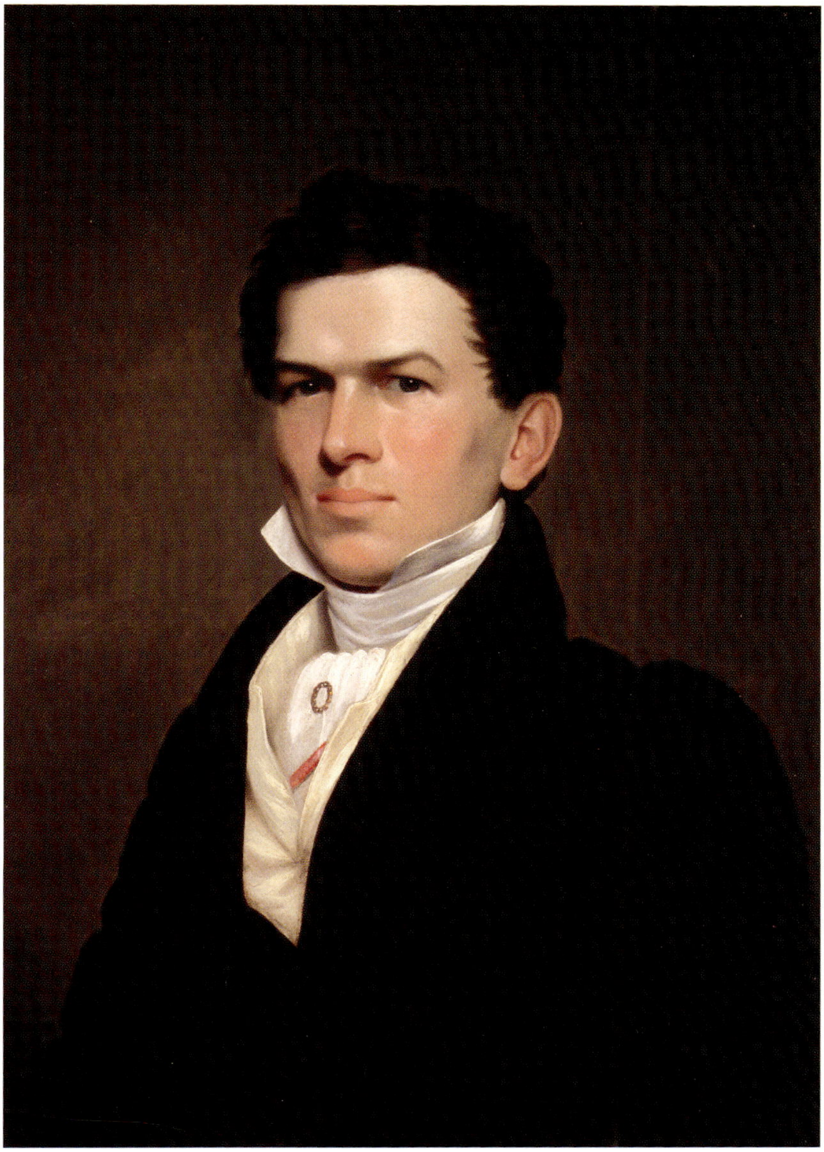

Portrait of Abraham Garland Randall
Oil on canvas
James Frothingham
ca. 1820–1825
J. J. Haverty Collection
High Museum of Art

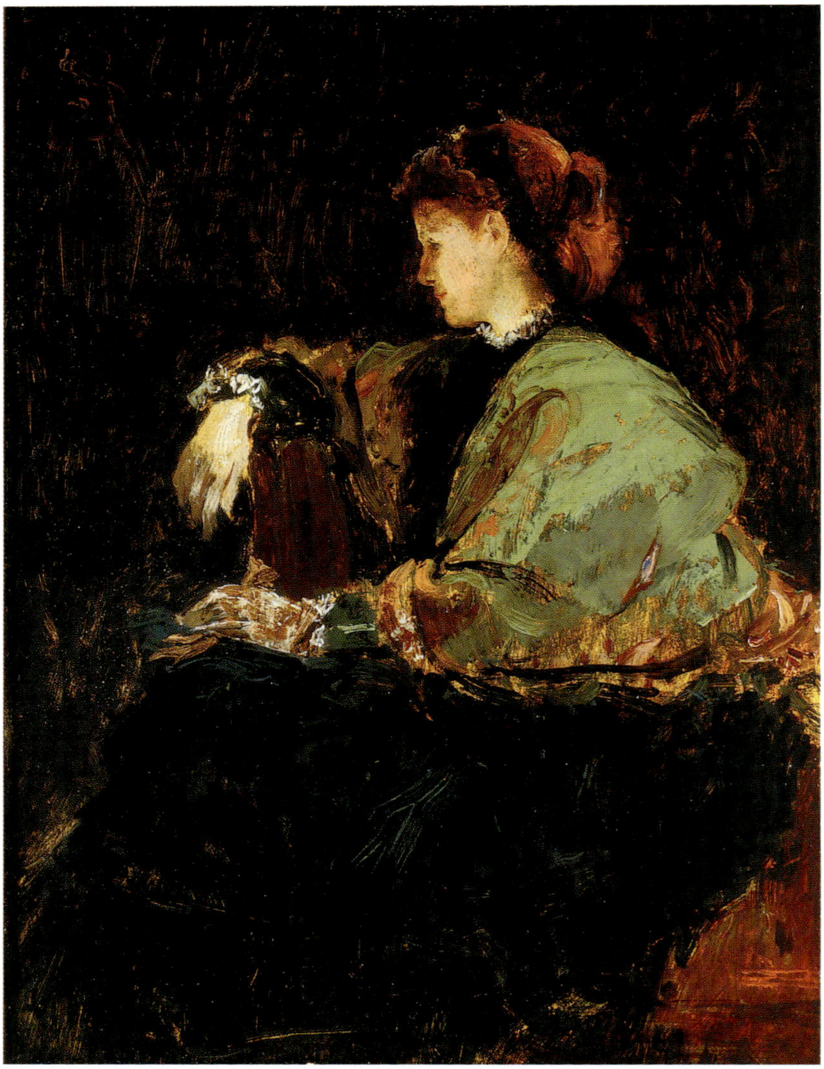

Meditation
Oil on wood panel
Alfred-Emile-Leopold Stevens
ca. 1870
J. J. Haverty Collection
High Museum of Art

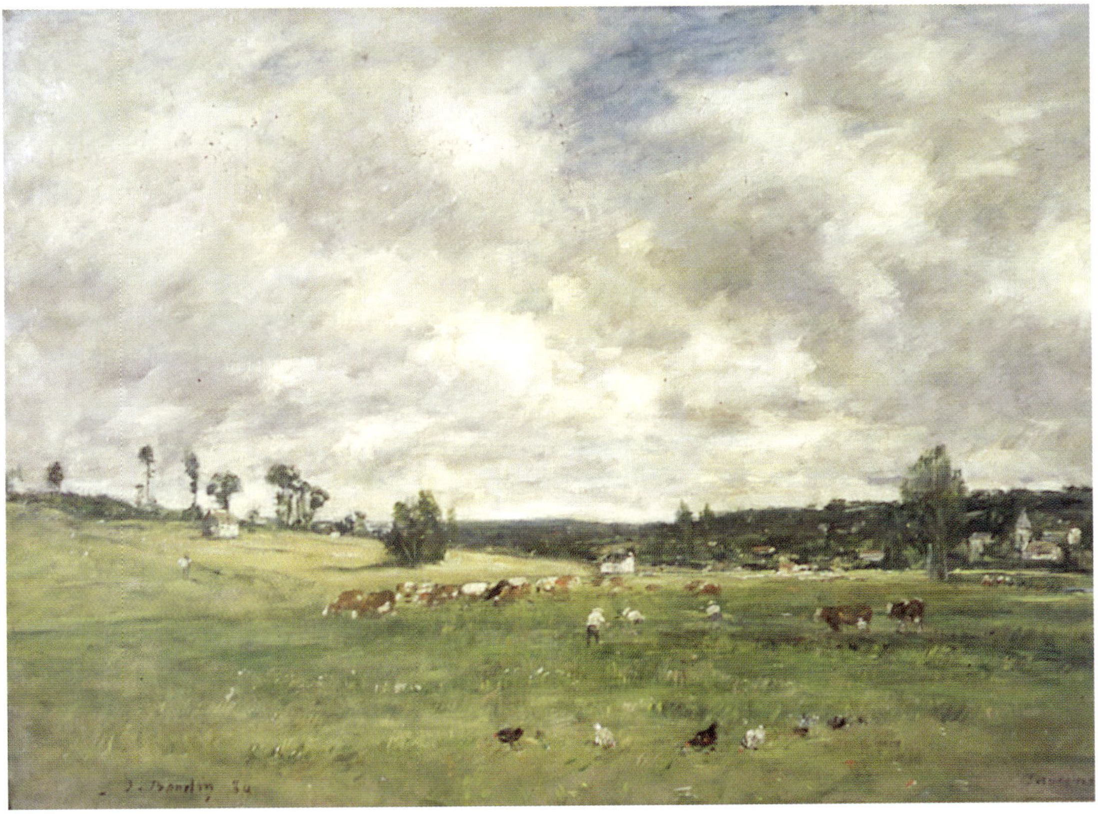

Landscape (Fervaques)
Oil on canvas
Eugène Boudin, 1884
J. J. Haverty Collection
High Museum of Art

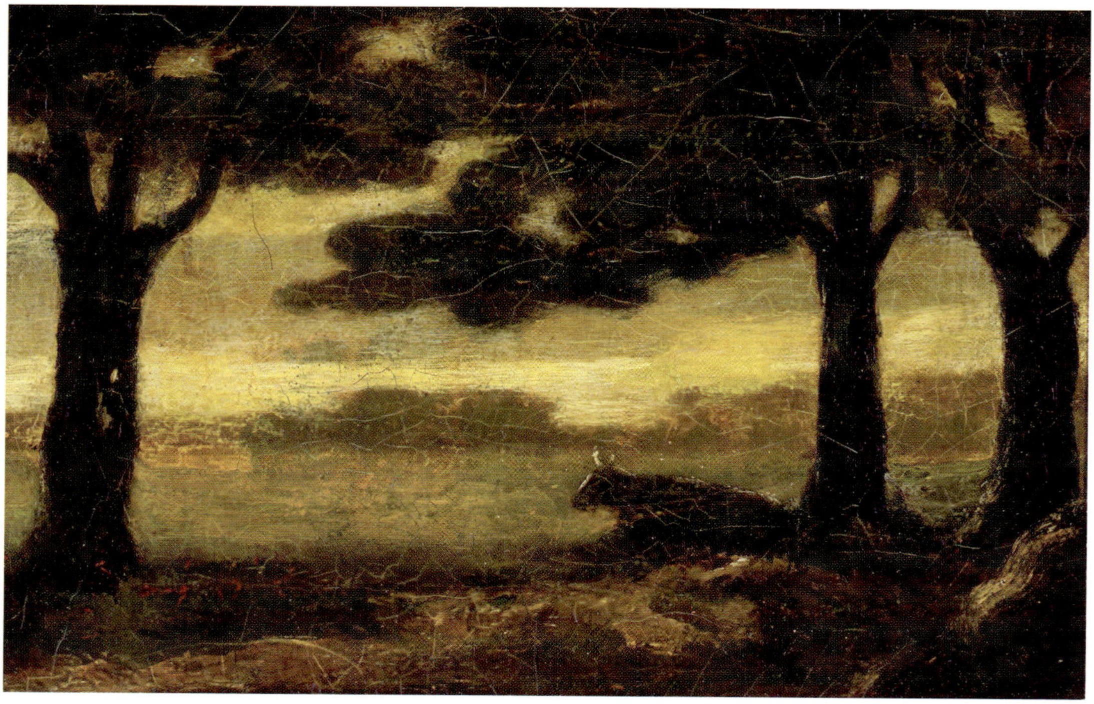

Landscape
Oil on canvas
Albert Pinkham Ryder,
1886
J. J. Haverty Collection
High Museum of Art

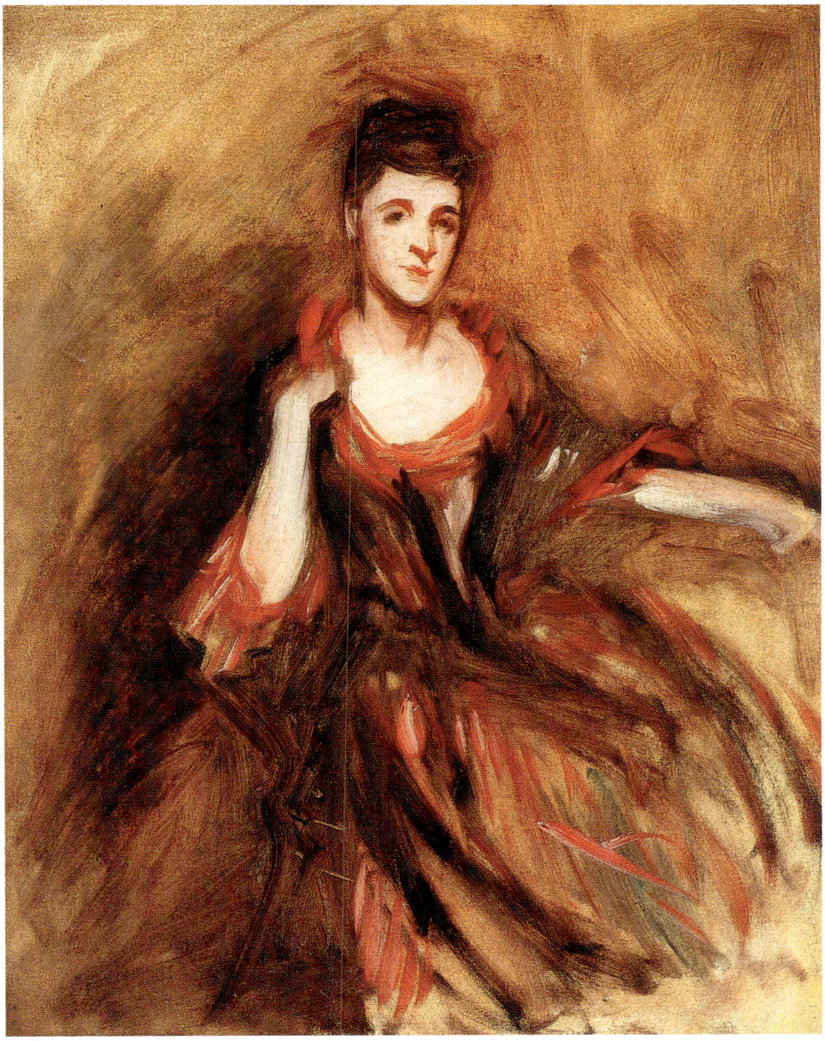

Sketch for the Portrait of Mrs. Manson
Oil on canvas
John Singer Sargent
ca. 1890
J. J. Haverty Collection
High Museum of Art

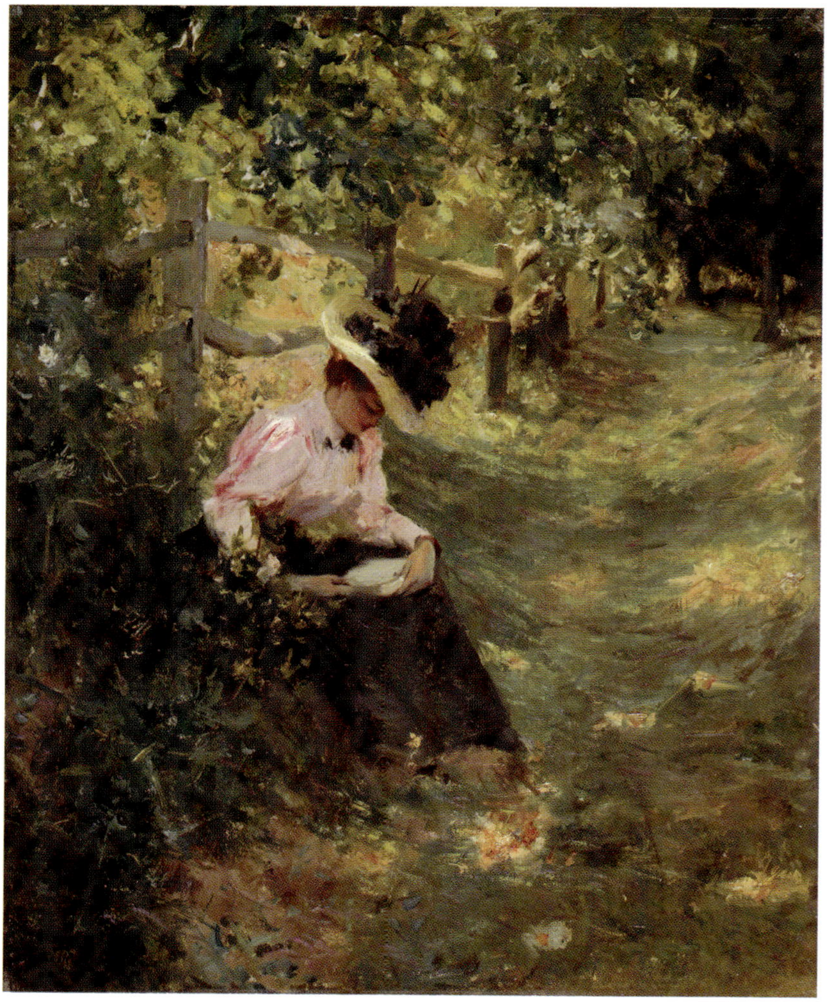

The Lane
Oil on canvas
Theodore Robinson
ca. 1893–1895
Gift of Miss Mary E. Haverty for the J. J. Haverty Collection
High Museum of Art

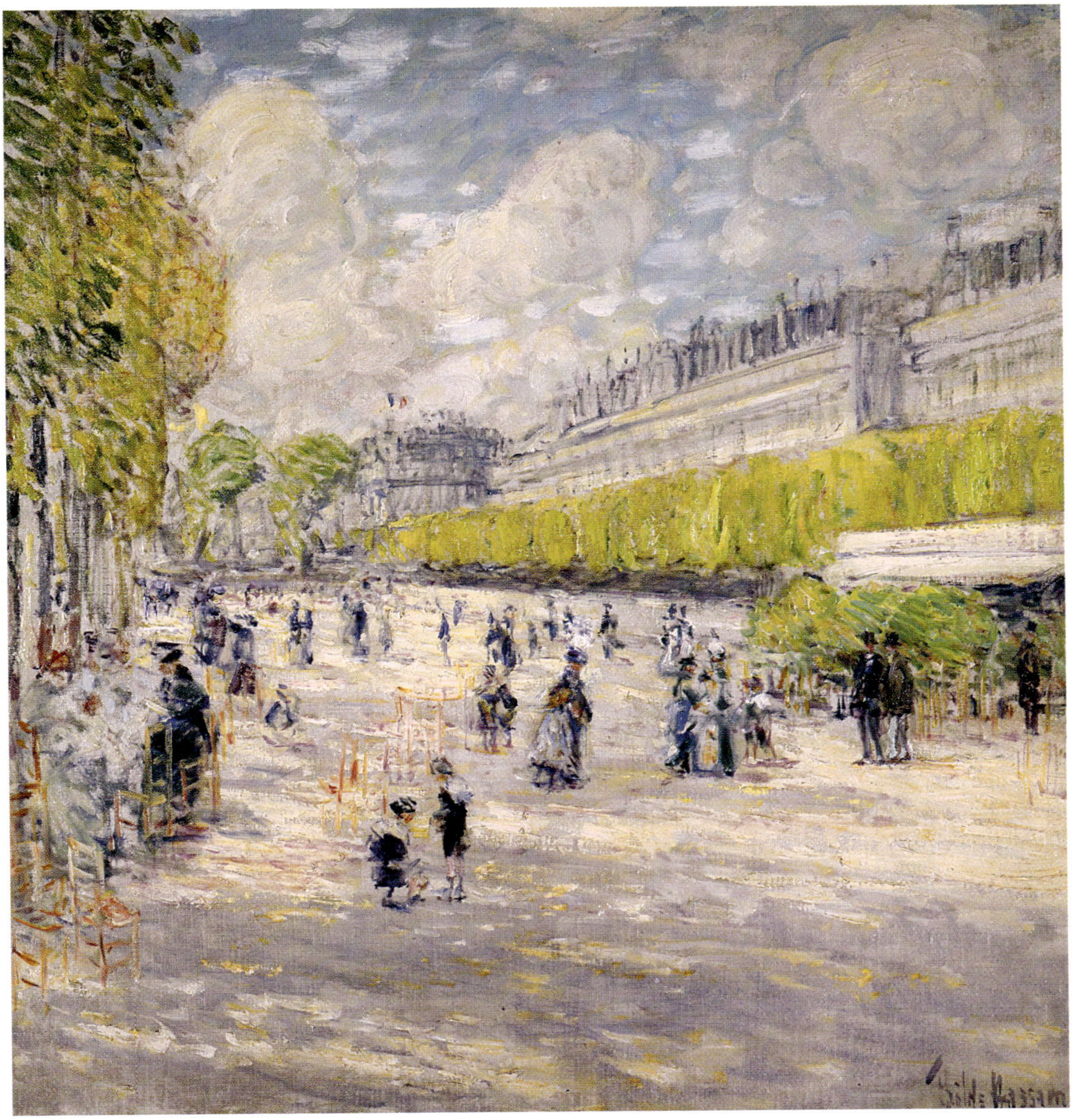

Tuileries Gardens

Oil on canvas

Childe Hassam, ca. 1897

Gift of Miss Mary E. Haverty for the J. J. Haverty Collection

High Museum of Art.

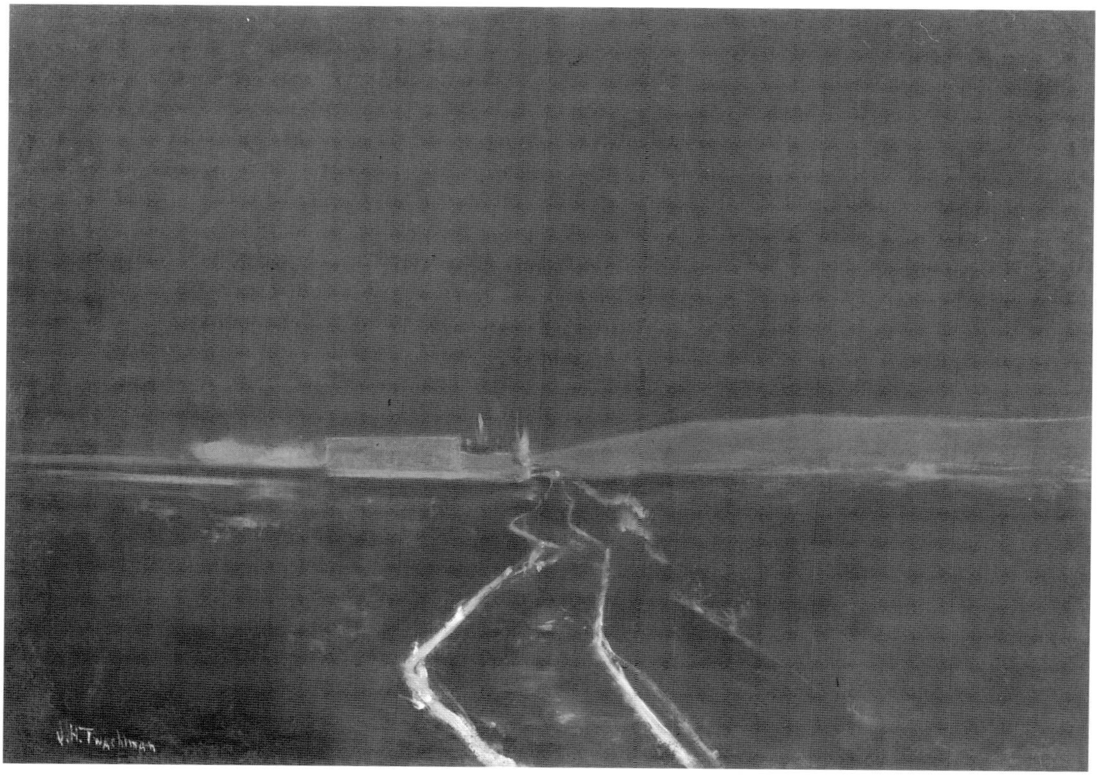

Along the River, Winter
Oil on canvas
John Henry Twachtman
J. J. Haverty Collection
High Museum of Art

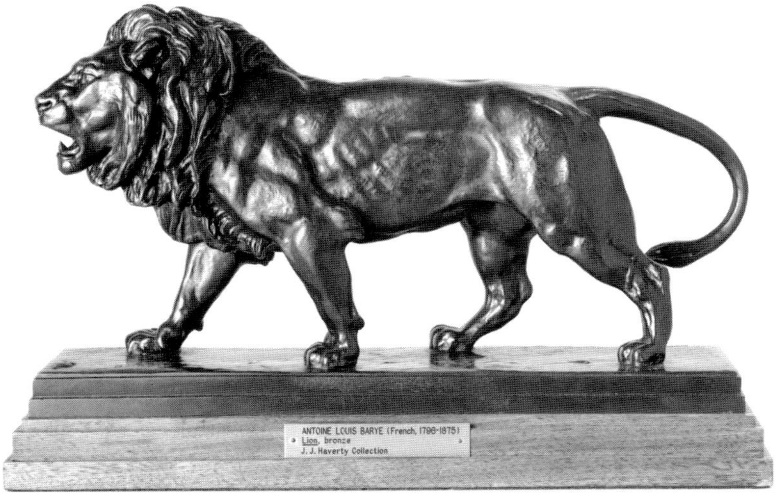

Walking Lion
Bronze
10 3/4" x 5" x 16 1/2"
Antoine-Louis Barye
nineteenth century
J. J. Haverty Collection
High Museum of Art.

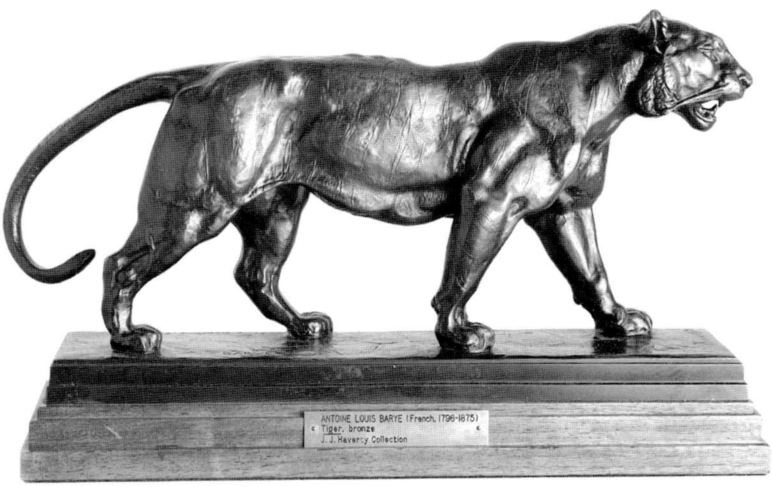

Walking Tiger
bronze
8 1/4" x 3 7/8" x 16 1/4"
Antoine-Louis Barye
nineteenth century
J. J. Haverty Collection
High Museum of Art.

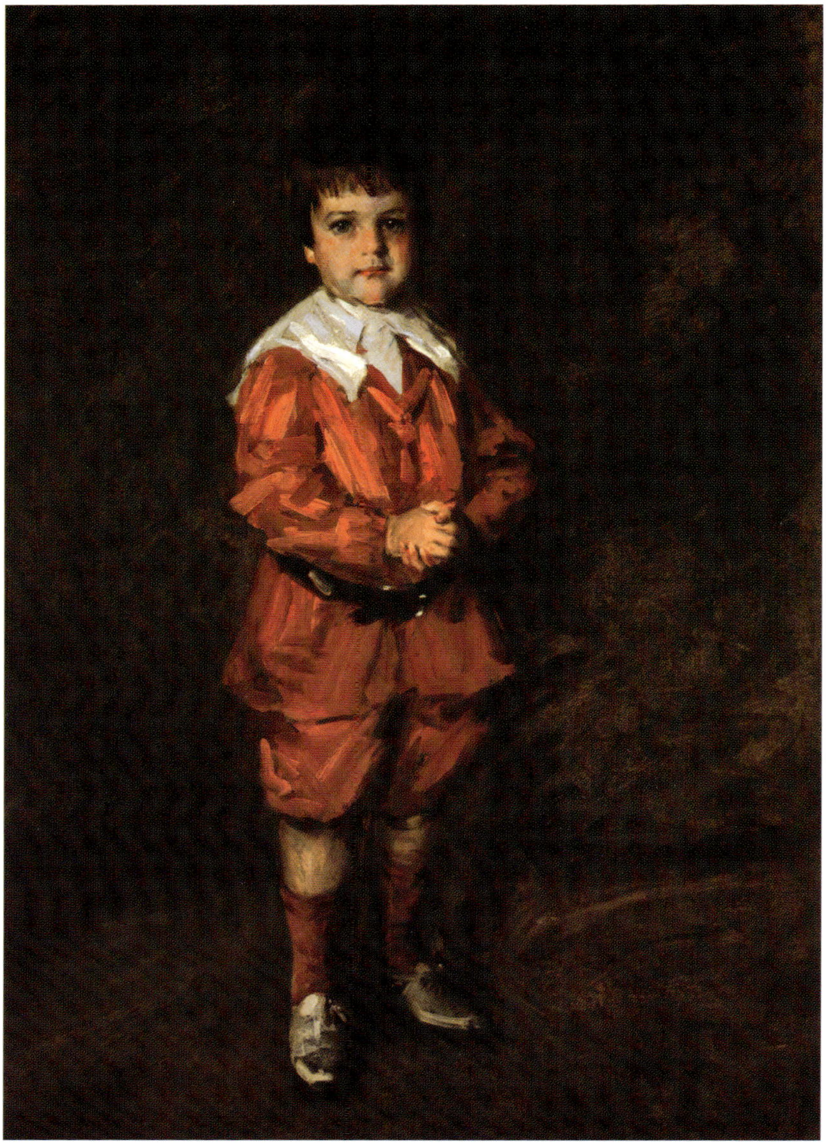

Portrait of Master Robert
Oil on canvas
William Merritt Chase
ca. 1902
J. J. Haverty Collection
High Museum of Art

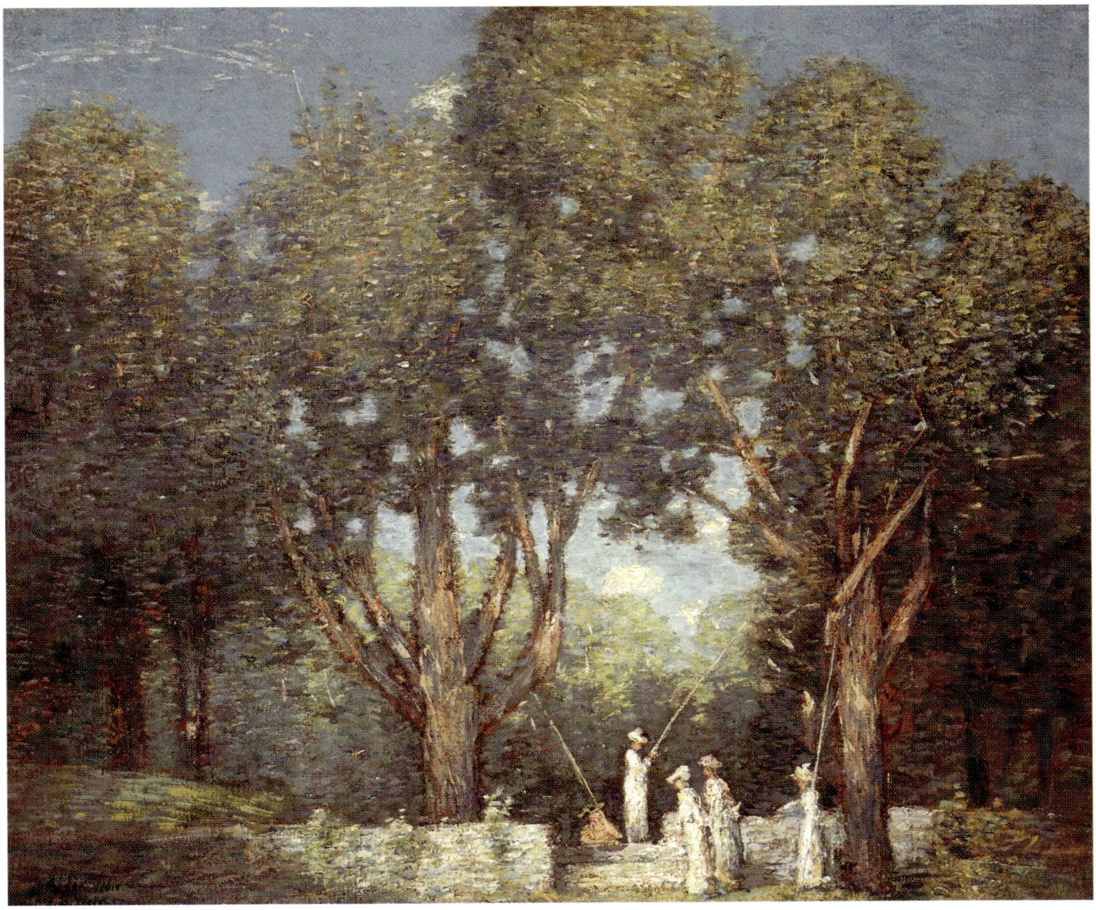

The Return of the Fishing Party

Oil on canvas

Julian Alden Weir

1906

Gift of Miss Mary E. Haverty for the J. J. Haverty Collection

High Museum of Art

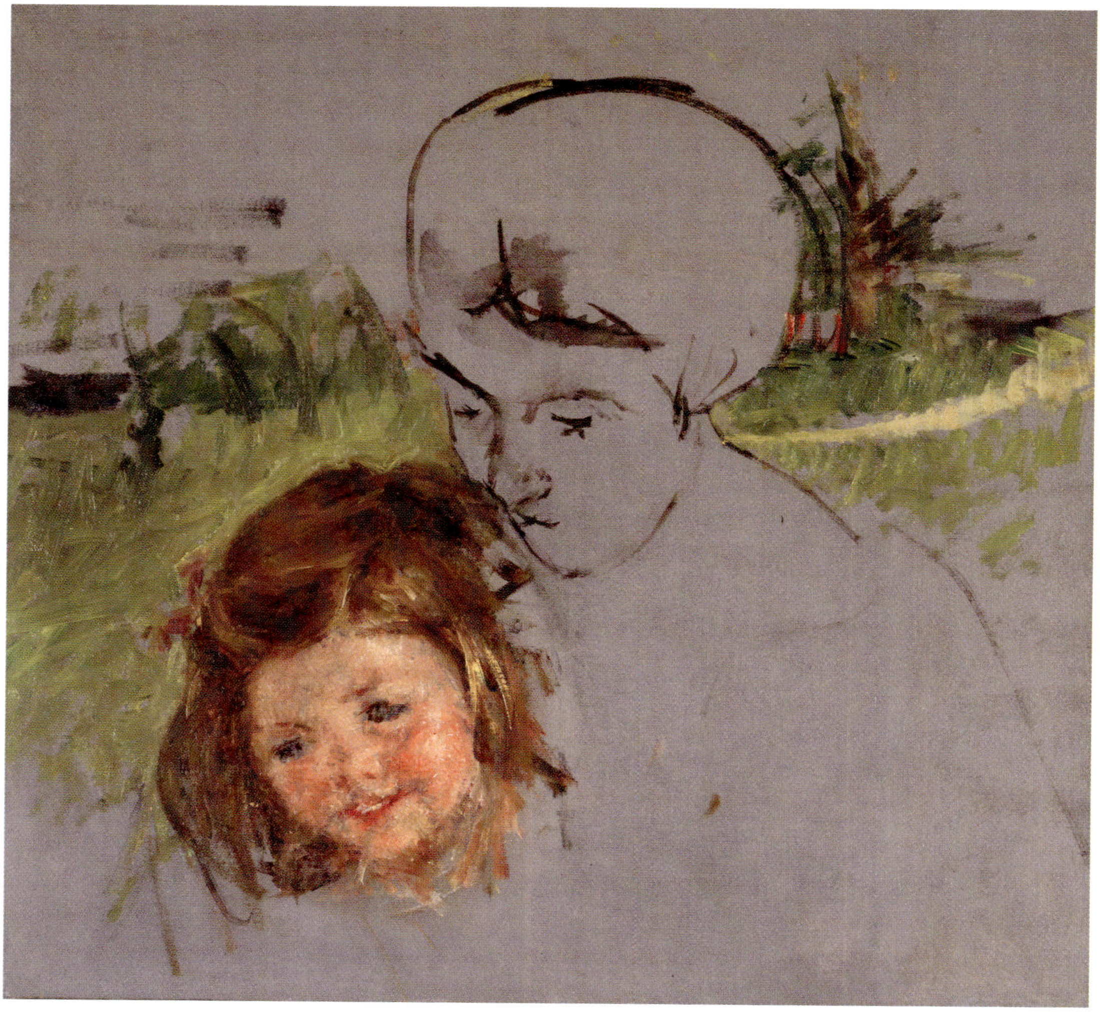

Preparatory Sketch for Mother and Child
Oil on canvas
Mary Cassatt
ca. 1906–1908
Gift in memory of Russell Bellman by his wife Katherine for the J. J. Haverty Collection
High Museum of Art

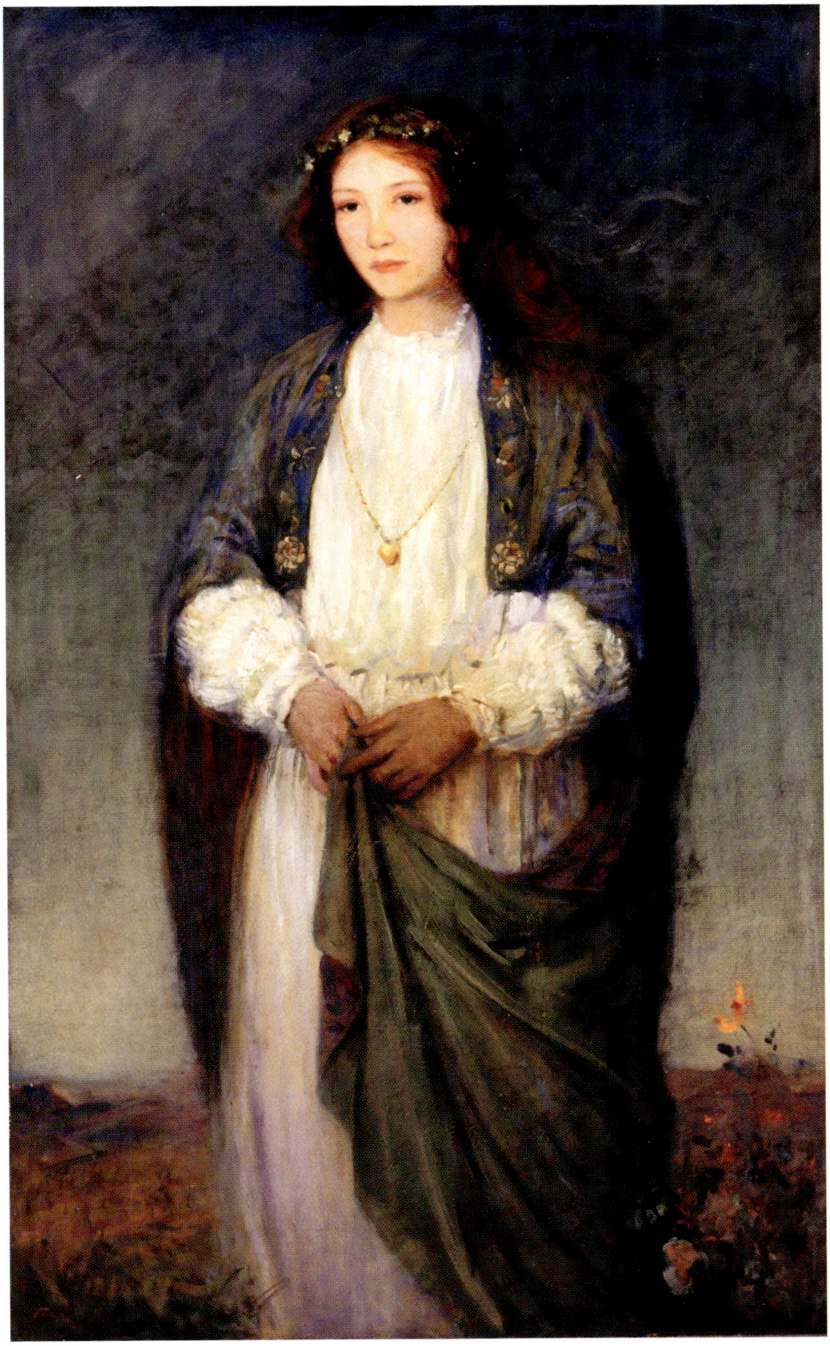

The Listener
Oil on canvas
Augustus Vincent Tack
ca. 1912
J. J. Haverty Collection
High Museum of Art

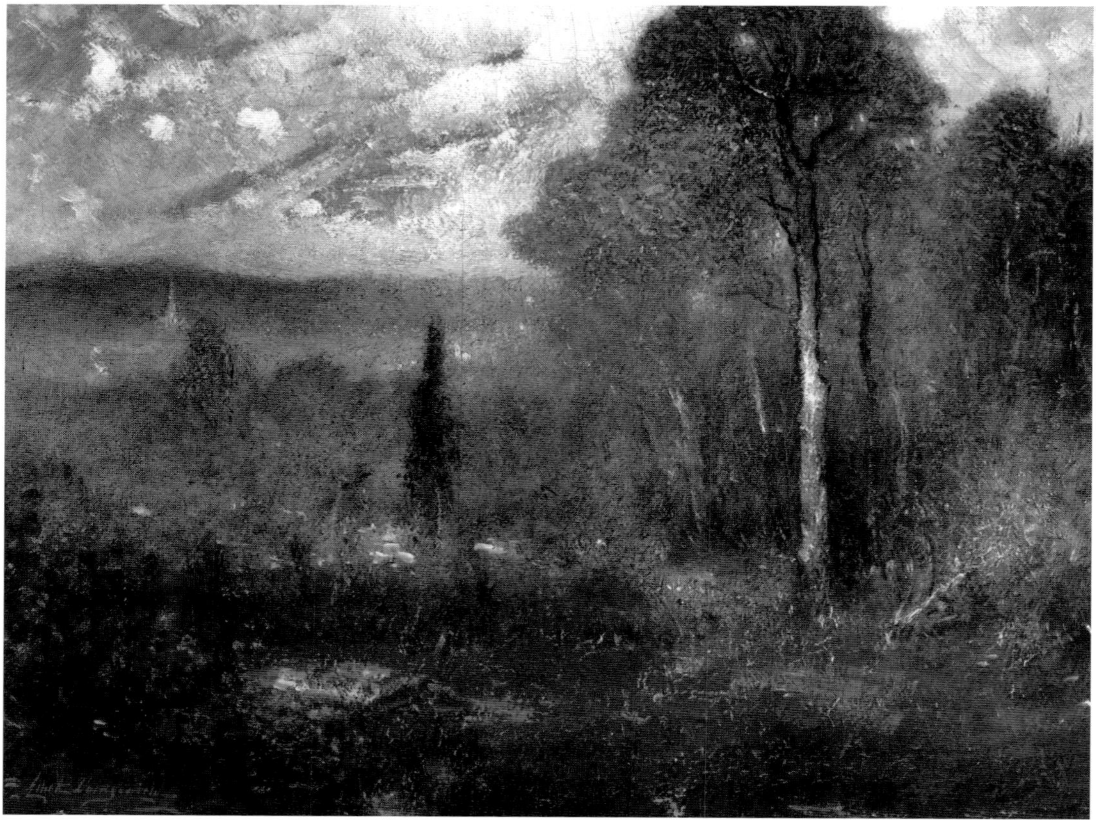

Blowing Rock
Oil on canvas
24 7/8" x 34 3/4"
Elliott Daingerfield
ca. 1923
J. J. Haverty Collection
High Museum of Art

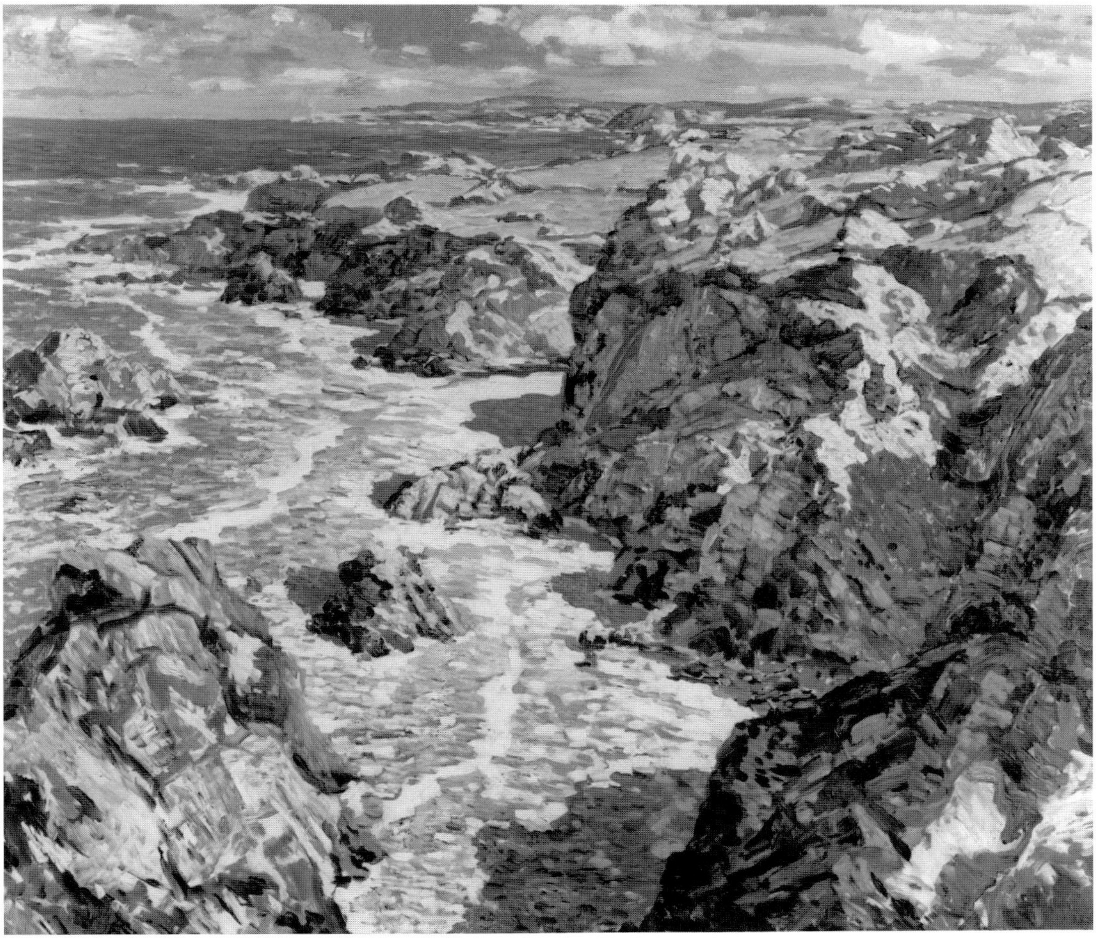

Sunlit Cove

Oil on canvas

Walter Elmer Schofield

1923

Gift of Miss Mary E. Haverty for the J. J. Haverty Collection

High Museum of Art

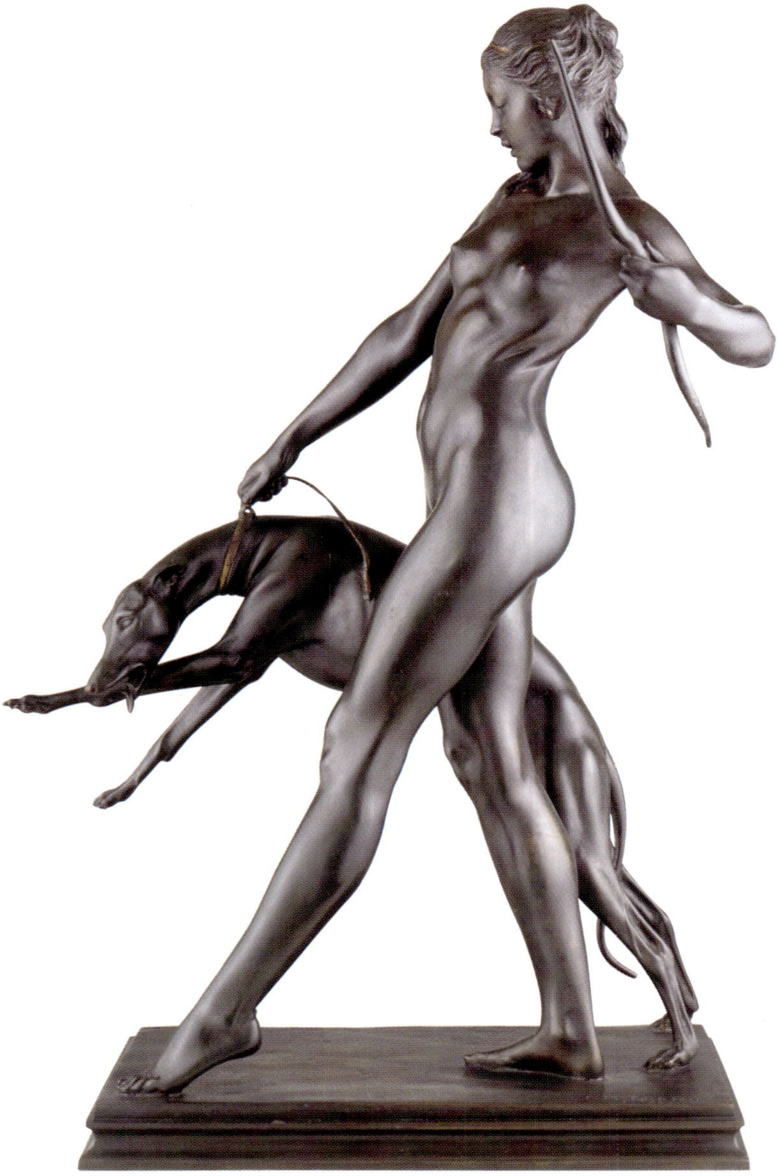

Diana and the Hound
Bronze
Edward McCartan
1923
J. J. Haverty Collection
High Museum of Art

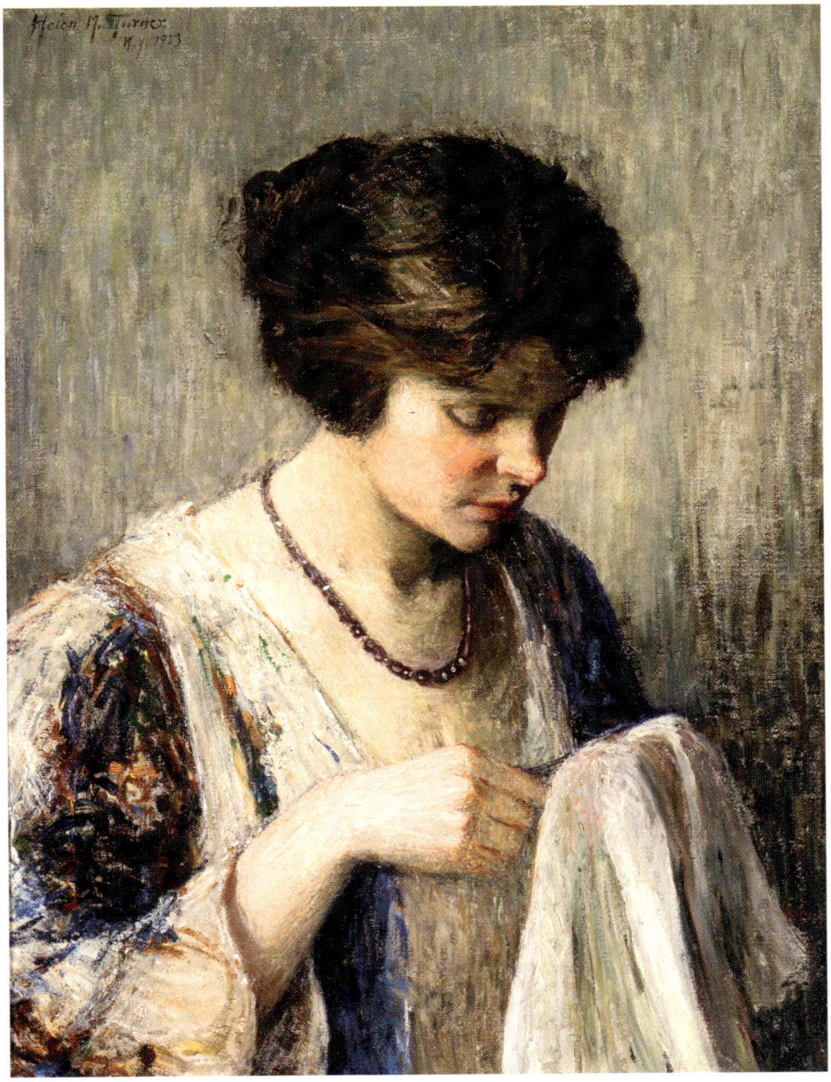

The Young Mother, No. 1
Oil on canvas
Helen Maria Turner
1923
Gift of Mr. And Mrs. Russel Bellman for the J. J. Haverty Collection
High Museum of Art

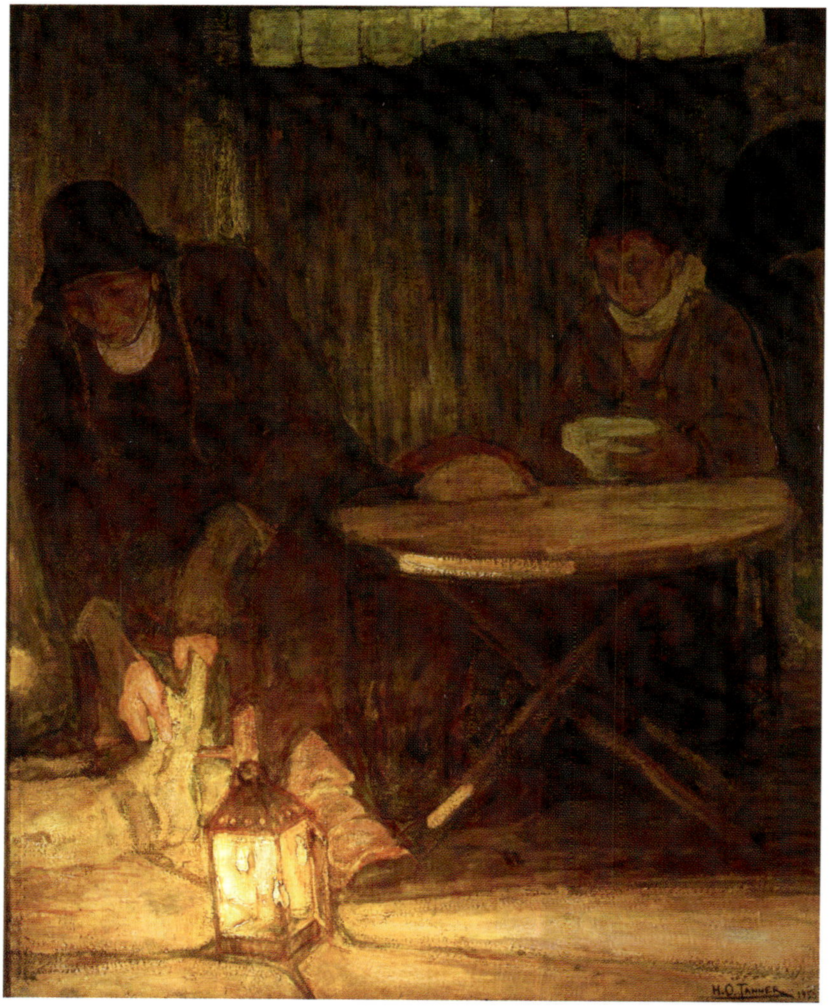

Etaples Fisher Folk
Tempera and oil on canvas
Henry Ossawa Tanner
1923
J. J. Haverty Collection
High Museum of Art

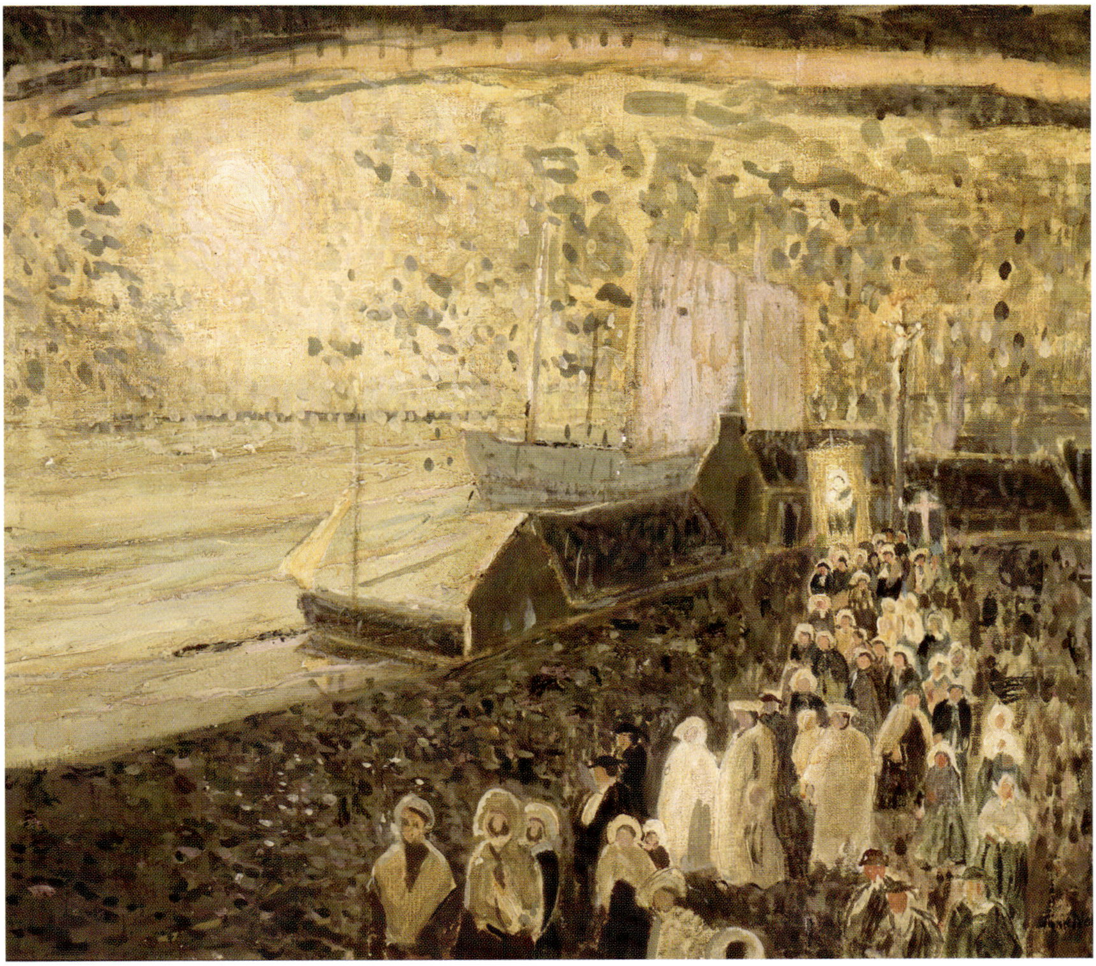

Benediction of the Sea
Oil on canvas
John Noble
ca. 1923–1924
Gift of Miss Mary E. Havery for the J. J. Haverty Collection
High Museum of Art

VILLA CLARE: PLATE 20

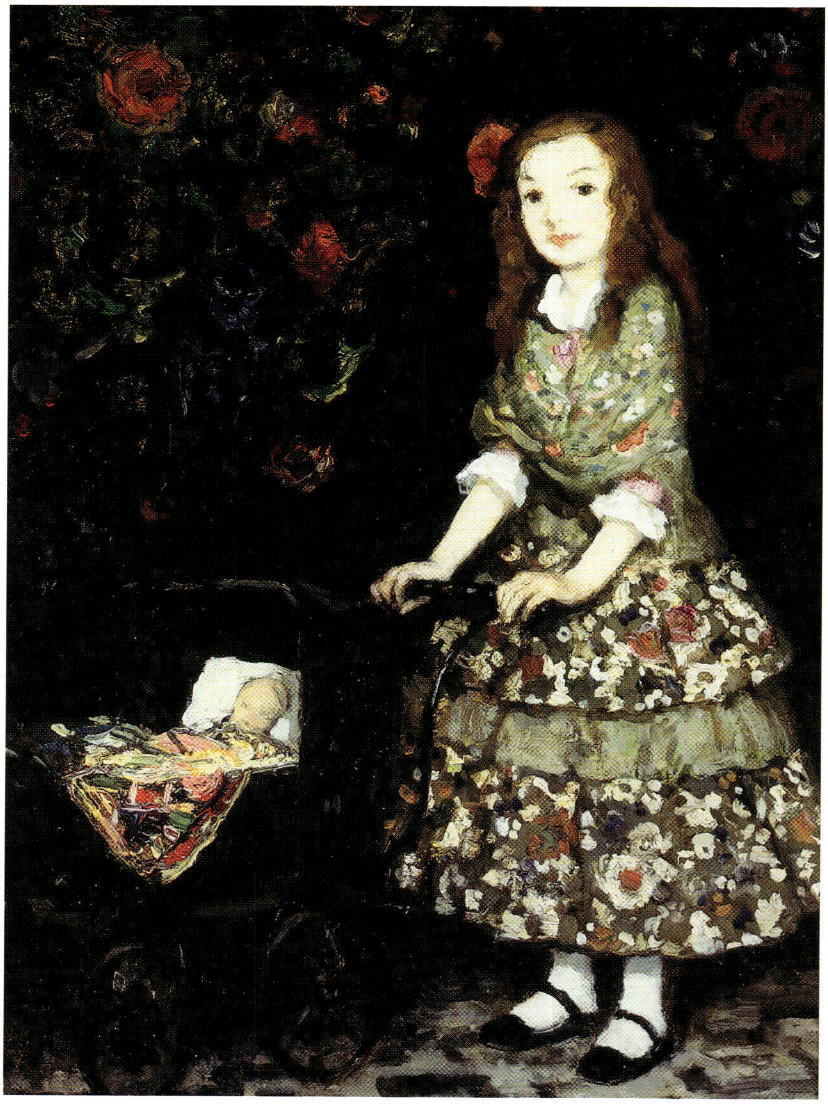

Doll Land Nurse
Oil on panel
Francis Luis Mora
ca. 1925
Gift of Miss Mary E. Haverty for the J. J. Haverty Collection
High Museum of Art

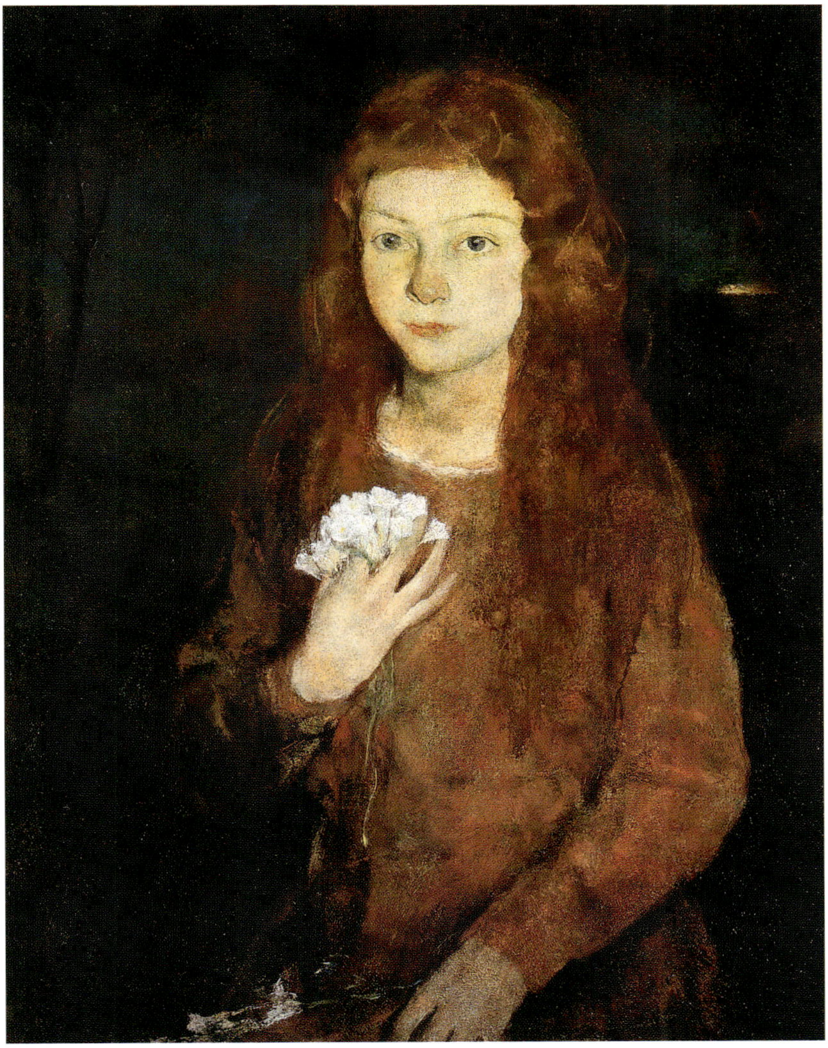

Spring Maiden
Oil on canvas
Charles Webster Hawthorne
ca. 1925
J. J. Haverty Collection
High Museum of Art

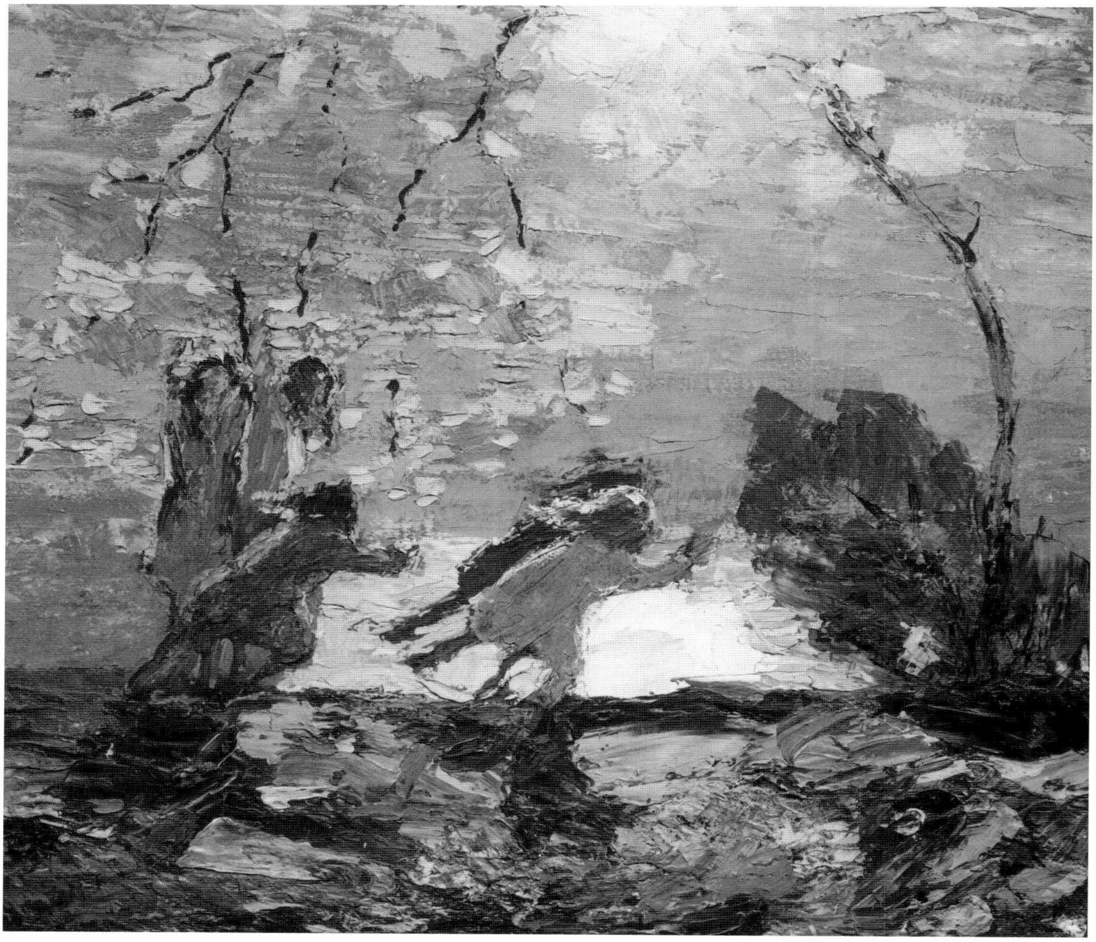

When the World Is Young
Oil on canvas
22" x 26"
Van Dearing Perrine
ca. 1925
Gift of Miss Mary E. Haverty for the J. J. Haverty Collection
High Museum of Art

VILLA CLARE: PLATE 23

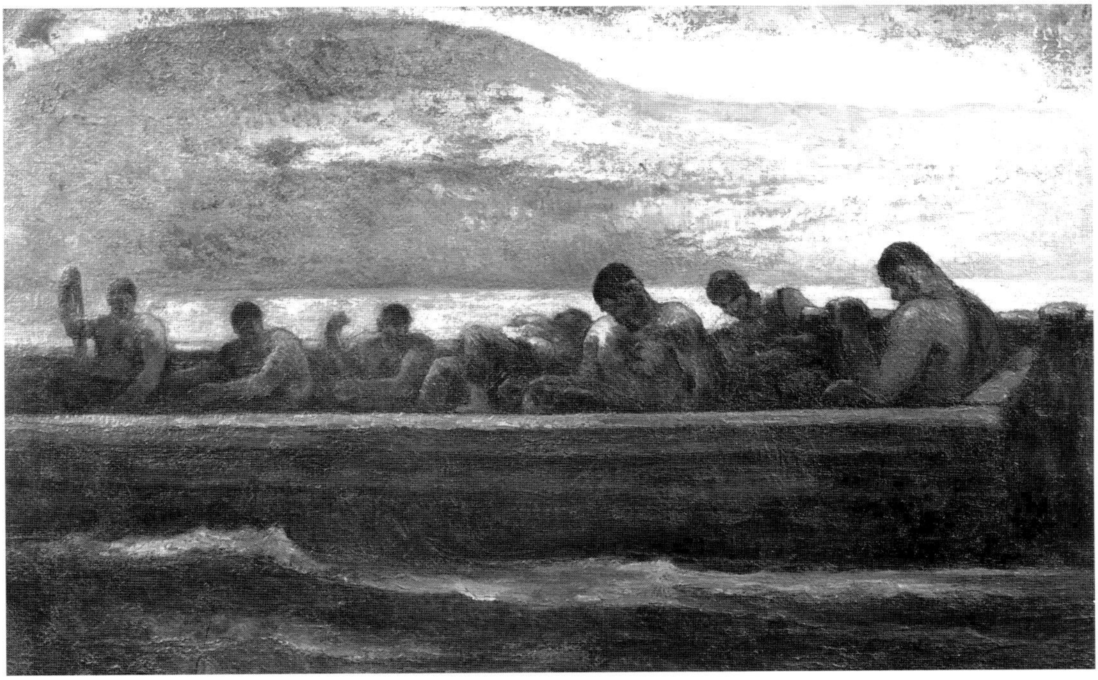

The Bargemen
Oil on canvas
23 1/4" x 37"
Eugene Higgins
ca. 1925
J. J. Haverty Collection
High Museum of Art

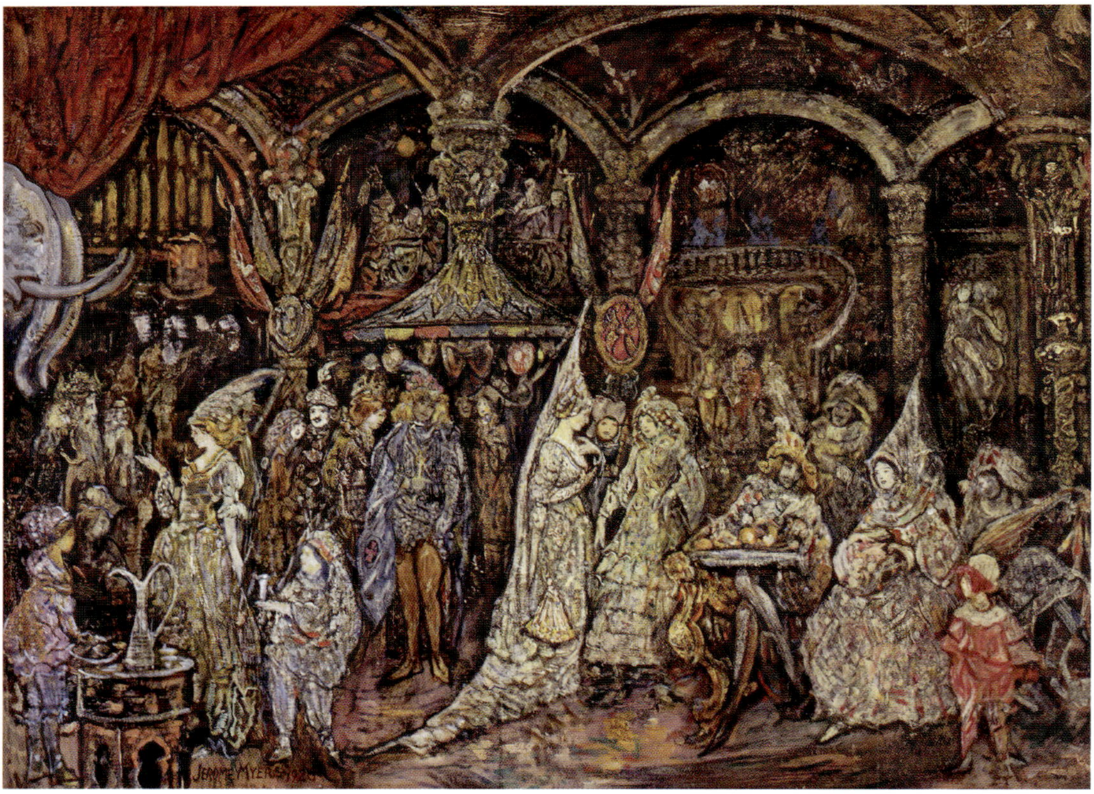

Medieval Ball
Oil on canvas
Jerome Myers
1926
J. J. Haverty Collection
High Museum of Art

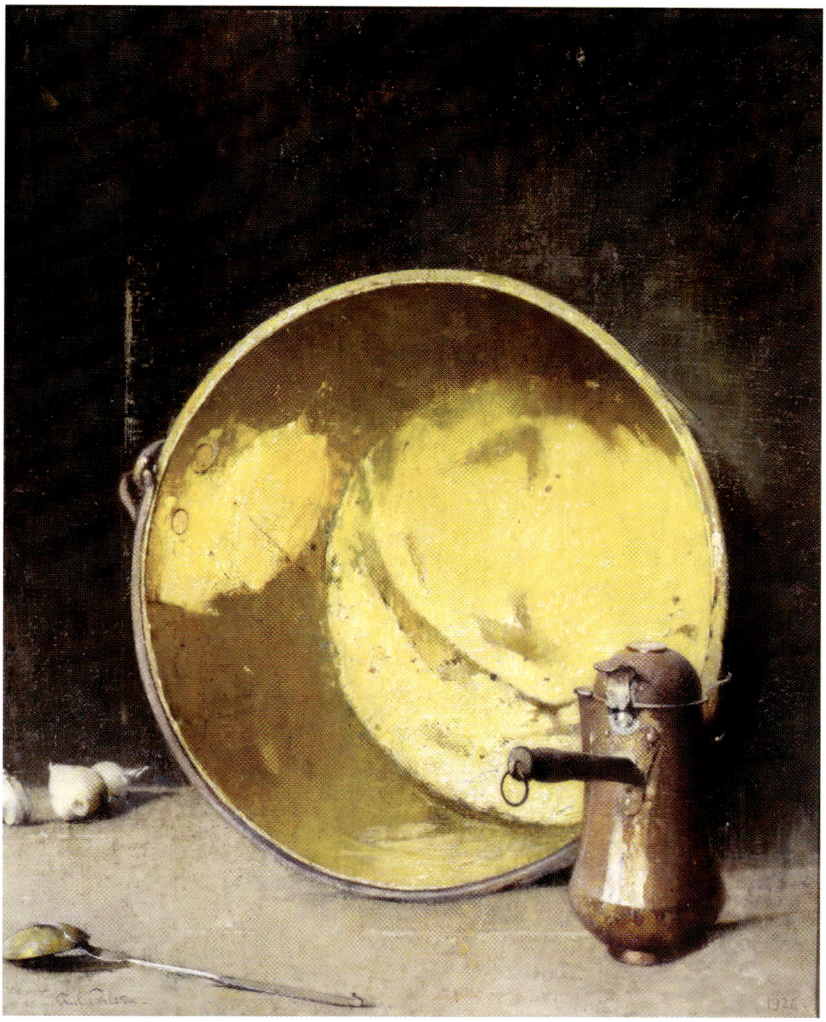

Still Life: Brass and Copper

Oil on canvas

Soren Emil Carlsen 1926

Gift of Miss Mary E. Haverty for the J. J. Haverty Collection

High Museum of Art

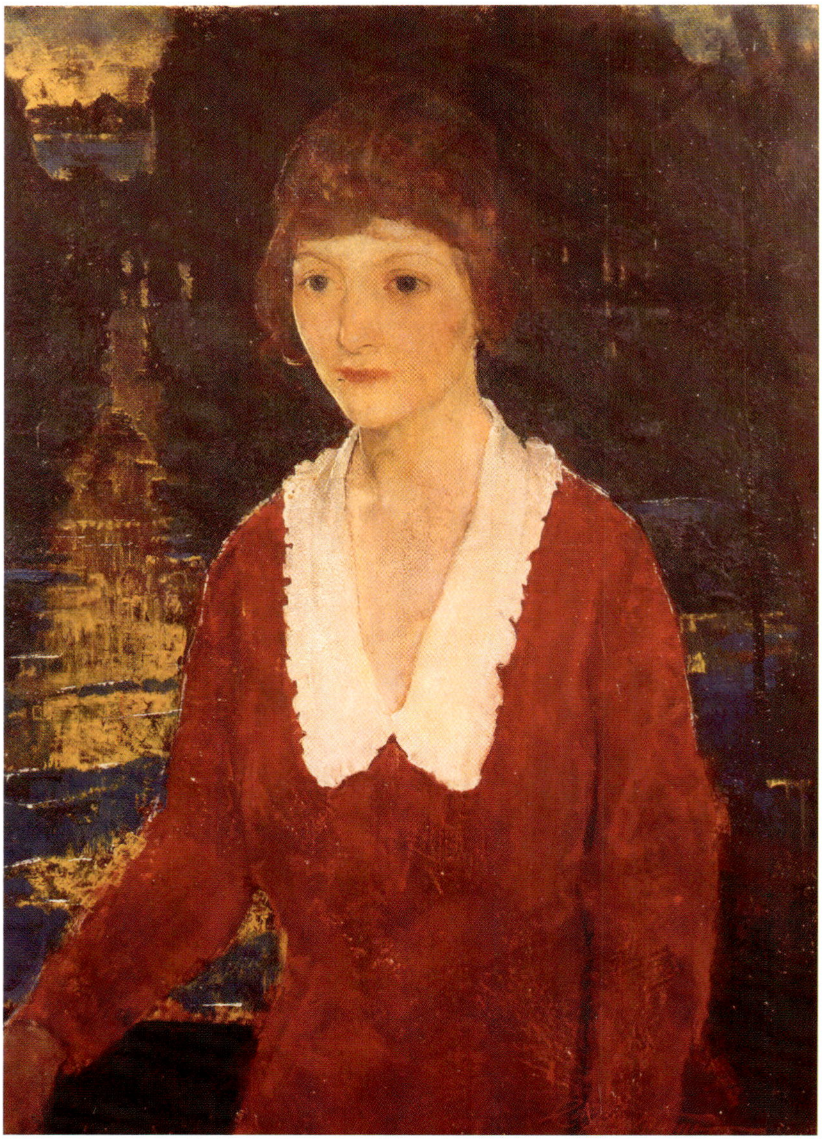

Portrait of Miss Wilson
Oil on paperboard
Charles Webster Hawthorne
ca. 1927
Gift of Miss Mary E. Haverty for the J. J. Haverty Collection
High Museum of Art

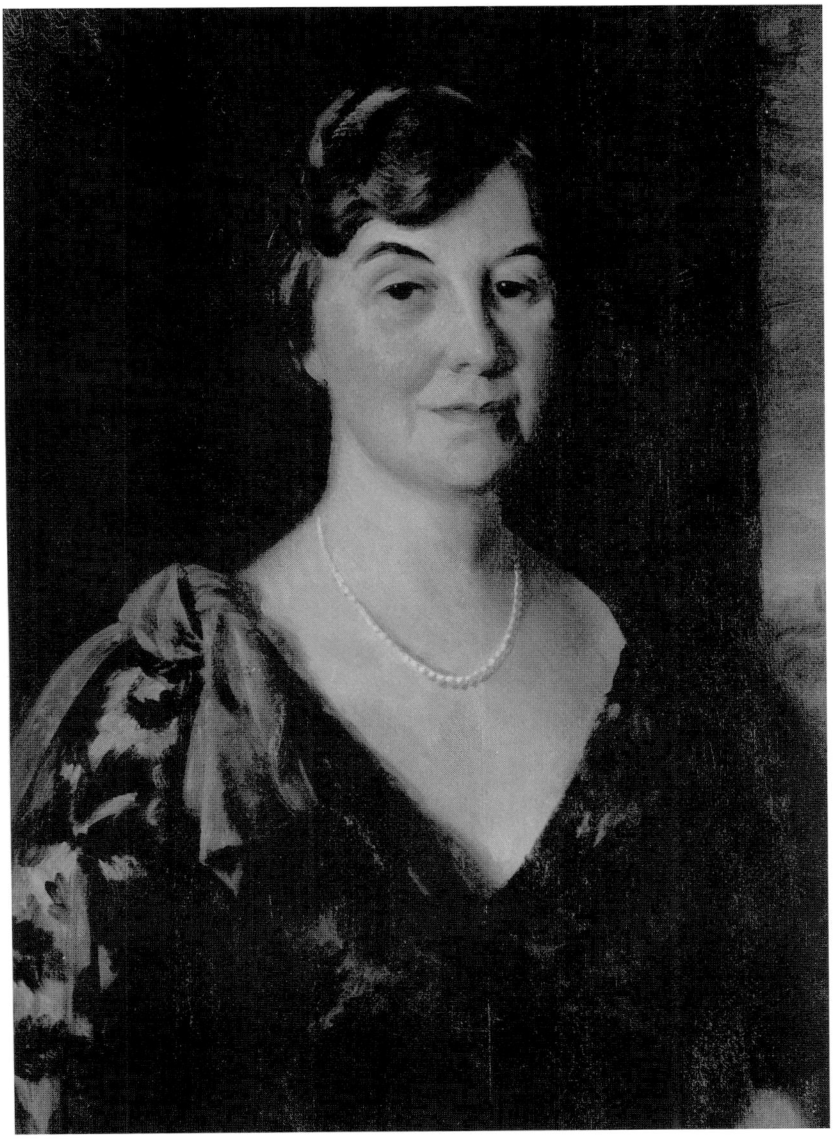

Portrait of
Ms. Mary Elizabeth Haverty

Oil on canvas

Paul Trebilcock

1930

Gift of Katherine Havery Bellman for the J. J. Haverty Collection

High Museum of Art

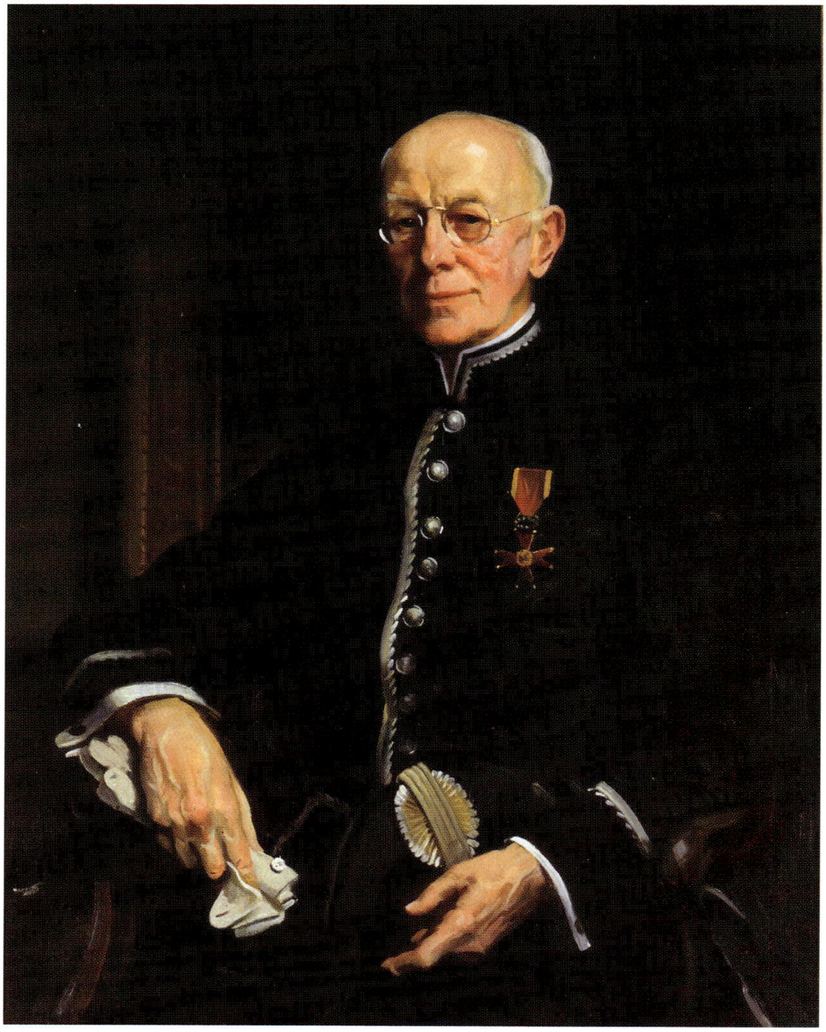

Portrait of James J. Haverty
Oil on canvas
John B. Johansen
1937
J. J. Haverty Collection
High Museum of Art

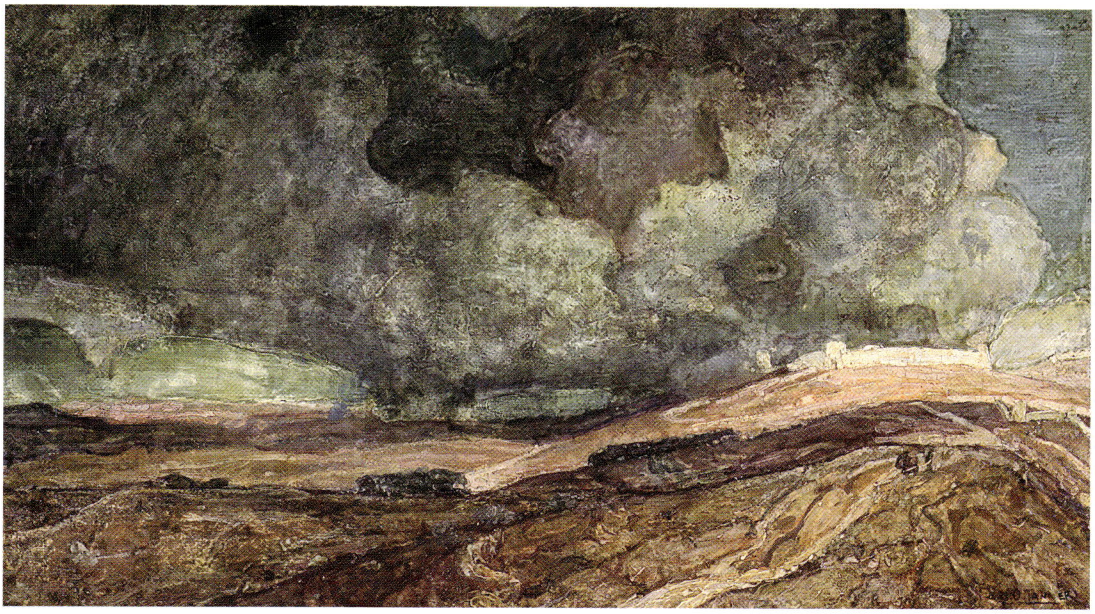

Destruction of Sodom and Gomorrah

Tempera and varnish

Henry Ossawa Tanner

1929

J. J. Haverty Collection

High Museum of Art

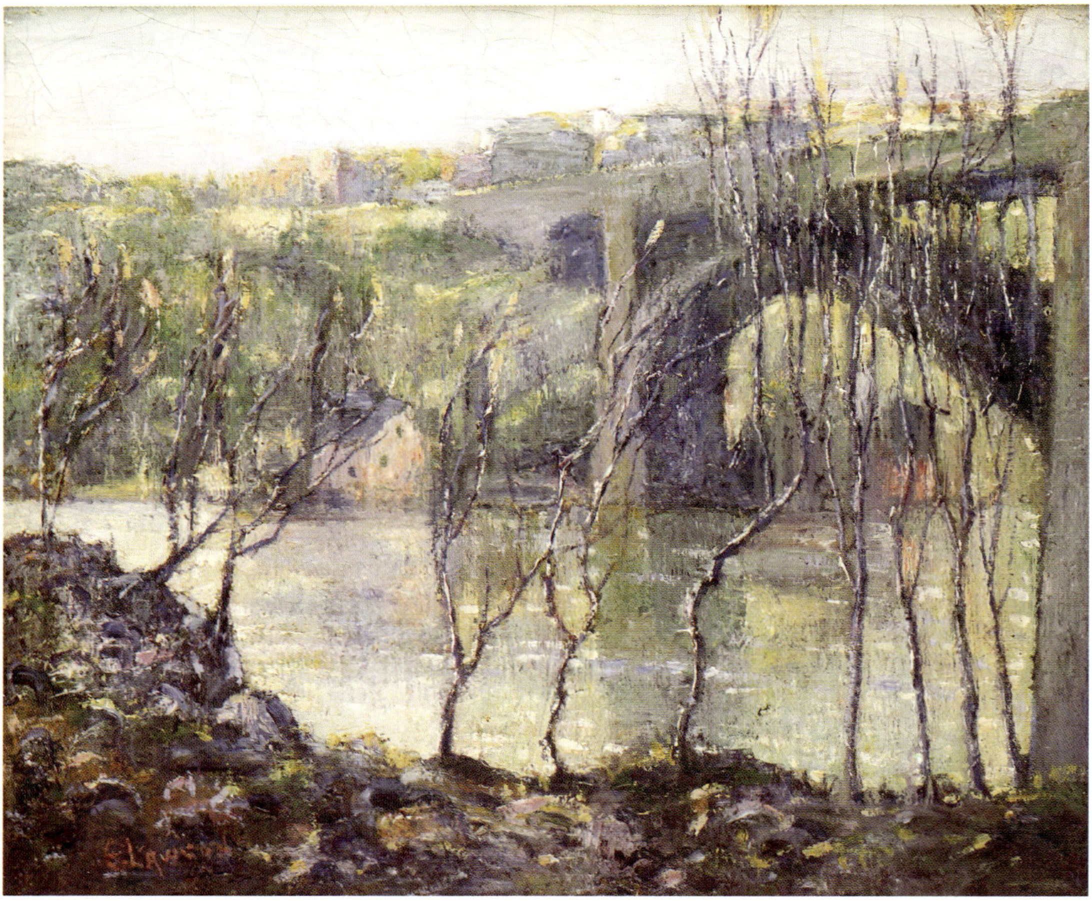

Washington Bridge, Harlem River

Oil on canvas

Ernest Lawson

J. J. Haverty Collection

High Museum of Art

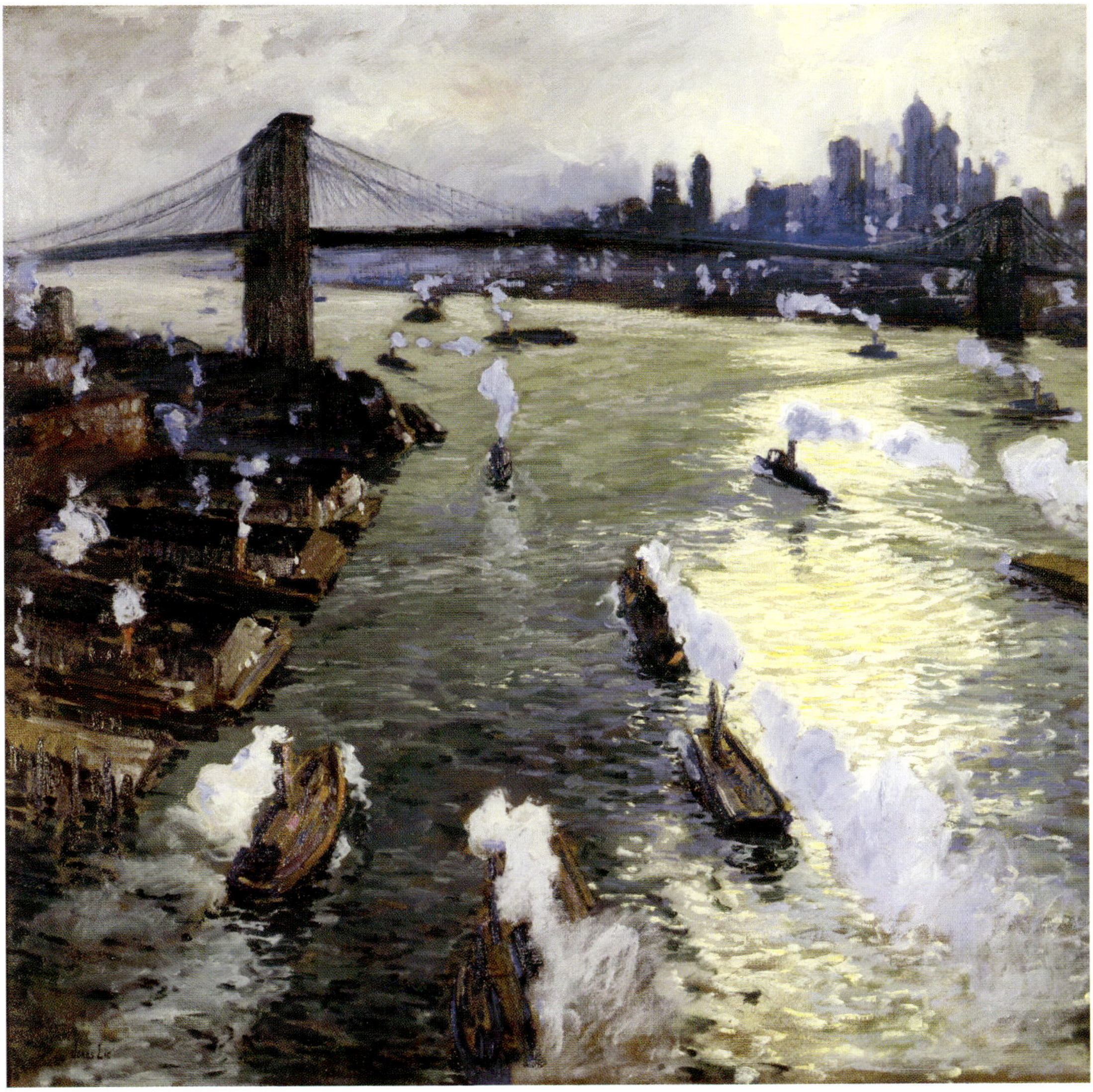

Path of Gold
Oil on canvas
Jonas Lie
J. J. Haverty Collection
High Museum of Art

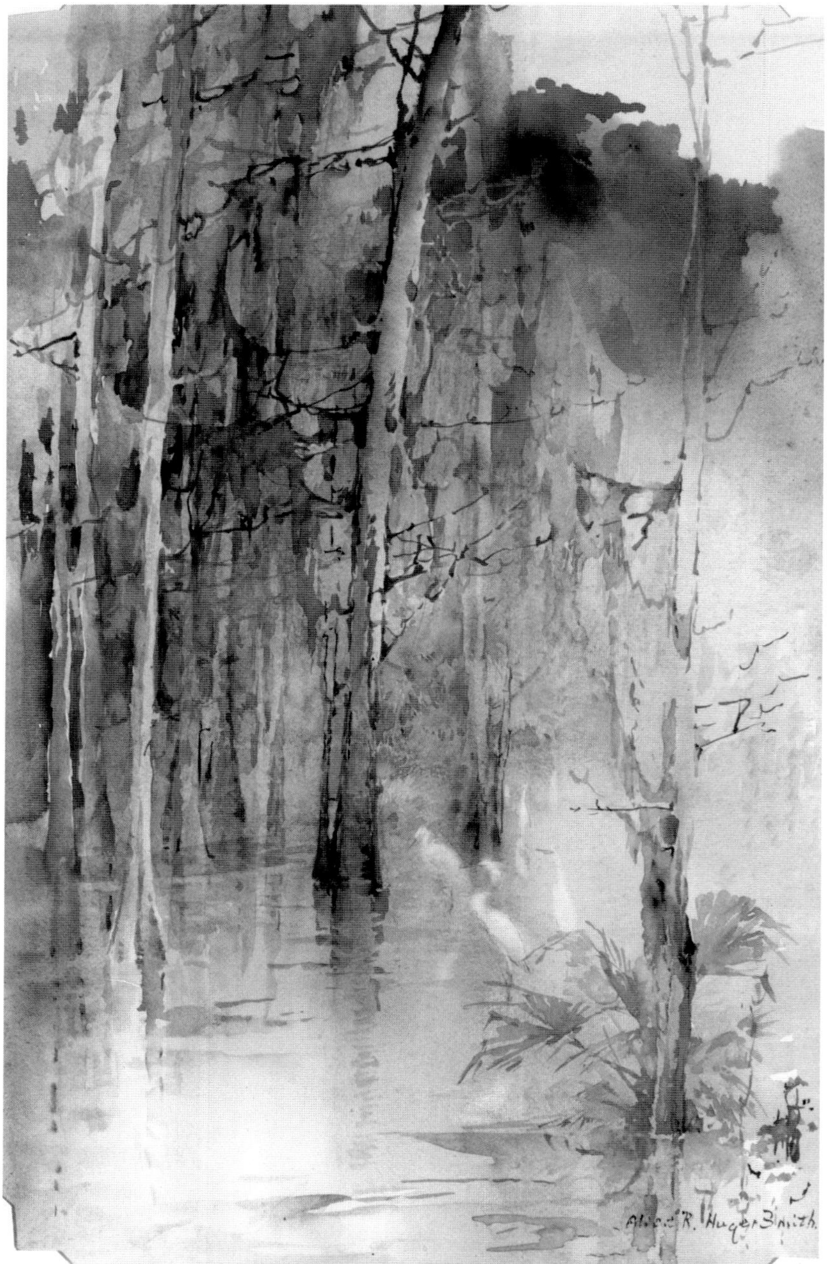

The Ashepoo Swamp
Watercolor on paper
20 3/4" x 31 3/4"
Alice Huger Smith
J. J. Haverty Collection
High Museum of Art

VILLA CLARE: PLATE 33

had signed its first full-time director, Roland McKinney. He was soon replaced by Lewis Skidmore. For the next two decades, Skidmore greatly expanded the High's programs, adding a new gallery called Memory Lane, a collection of paintings given by relatives or friends in memory of their departed relatives.

During the 1930s, the High Museum managed to keep open its doors and continue to operate an art school on the second floor of the old High house. Given the weak condition of the local economy during the Great Depression, raising money for additional expansion was out of the question, and many of Skidmore's projects were delayed or canceled. Skidmore successfully held together a core group of members and financial supporters, including Haverty. At a time when traveling exhibitions were scarce and the infant museum had few resources, Haverty tried to sustain public interest in the arts any way possible. If that meant opening the doors to his own home so the people of Atlanta could enjoy fine paintings, then he was glad to oblige. On most Sunday afternoons, he opened the doors of Villa Clare to visitors, serving tea and light snacks to anyone who wanted to come by and see his personal collection. Other members of the Haverty family were unhappy with the idea of opening their beloved Villa Clare to everyone in town. But Haverty understood that the flame of art in Atlanta could be easily extinguished.

For more than seven decades, Haverty had seen too much change to take anything for granted, including the city's new cultural progress. He had seen the easy prosperity of the antebellum South turn to ashes and then be rebuilt—at least in Atlanta—in a pattern of industrial America. He had seen the emergence of airplanes, radio, and mass communication. And before his eyes, Peachtree Street evolved from a muddy gas-lit Indian trail choked with beasts of burden into a brightly lit and smoothly paved thoroughfare for automobiles and busses. Reflecting on his own story, Haverty was a flesh-and-blood example of progress: a laborer's son who had become a millionaire retailer with the best art collection in the South. And then there was the sudden emergence of the High museum, which exemplified the new Atlanta.

So it was with an uneasy sense of satisfaction that Haverty saw the new High Museum, which he described proudly as a "cultural shrine which will stimulate interest in things beautiful, a home where Atlanta's children and her children's children may study and learn beauty as it is portrayed by master minds and talent."[80] Haverty had no idea how Atlanta's first museum would develop. But he did have a clear idea of what was needed to succeed, and he brought the wherewithal and determination to make the vision of a permanent institution of the arts in Atlanta into a reality.

"The object of art is not only to give pleasure, as many are apt to assume, but to express high spiritual realities."

J. J. Haverty, 1927

The Final Years

Some might call it the luck of the Irish. Others might credit foresight. But there's no doubt J. J. Haverty dodged financial disaster during his final years by the narrowest of margins. As it turned out, despite some minor setbacks, he prospered throughout the Great Depression and took advantage of a decline in asset prices to add to his burgeoning art collection. Like most everyone else during the late 1920s, J. J. Haverty was blissfully unaware of the Great Depression lurking ahead. Swept up in the optimistic spirit of the day, he aggressively expanded his business operations. The self-made Haverty had a high tolerance for risk and by the late 1920s had borrowed significantly to purchase—among many other things—real estate, both residential and commercial. He bought vast amounts of land in the Buckhead section of Atlanta, sensing growth in the pine-covered hills and ravines just to the north of Villa Clare. His estate later sold much of the land he purchased to the Westminster Schools, among other buyers.

As a man who embraced bold ideas and initiatives, Haverty was not afraid to try his hand at the great game of high-rise commercial real estate, along with his old friend and former furniture business partner A. G. Rhodes. Although his health was fading by the mid-1920s, Rhodes was not one to pass on opportunity. Atlanta businesses needed room to grow, and the city's old Beaux Arts buildings from pre-World War I (such as the Healey building) were no longer adequate for the city's ambitious new class of office tenants. Atlanta's up-and-coming businesses wanted larger offices and conference rooms, better views, more efficient heating systems as well as the prestige of an address in a distinctive and visible skyscraper. The race was on to build the tallest building in Atlanta, and Haverty and Rhodes were determined to win it.

'An Unusually Handsome Landmark'

In 1924, Rhodes and Haverty began to plan for a "modern, up to date, fireproof office building: the cost of the same to be $750,000." The Rhodes-Haverty Realty and Investment Co. picked a site adjacent to the Candler building, which had been developed and named after one of the founders of the Coca-Cola Company. For their proposed tower at 134 Peachtree Street, Rhodes and Haverty hired Francis P. Smith, student of the noted American architect Paul Cret and former chairman of the Georgia Tech architecture department. As a partner in the firm Pringle & Smith, he drafted plans for a daring steel-framed design with an art deco flair. In the original design, the top of the building was to be crowned in terra cotta with three arches under a corbelled gabled. But the architects modified the design to address concerns that the tower would cast a shadow across the streetscape.

According to an interview, the architects published in the October 1928 *City Builder*, the still-unfinished building would "be of distinct American design, one that will be an unusually handsome landmark for the upper Peachtree...the very latest word in office building and the first of its kind in the South. The ground floor on the street frontages will be devoted to store space...and an arcade is planned for the north side of the building."[81]

Speaking while the building was under construction, Haverty emphasized its aesthetic importance: "Beauty should be combined with utility, thereby developing standards of culture in architecture which will represent the energy imagination and aspirations of the American spirit.... Atlanta is looked upon as the center of culture in the South, and in this new building is to be illustrated that spirit of culture which belongs to the South."

A.G. Rhodes died in 1928, but work continued on the building until its completion in October 1929, the same month as the "Black Monday" stock market crash that led to the Great Depression. It was the city's tallest building (and would remain so for decades). A historical marker on the location today describes the building as "An important transition in the city's skyscraper development on the eve of the Great Depression." But after the grand opening, the glory for the developers was short lived. The Rhodes-Haverty building was nearly vacant for years. Haverty was able to survive this potentially crippling financial setback and stay solvent during the Great Depression in large part because of another very fortunate business transaction that occurred in late 1929, just as the doors to his high rise property were being opened.

Dodging the Crash

As J. J. Haverty continued to pursue risky investments, his eldest son Clarence became increasingly concerned. By the late 1920s, Clarence Haverty was in his forties and was running the furniture business day to day, even though J. J. Haverty retained the title of president until 1937. As a prominent executive with a high profile (he was elected to the Atlanta city council for a while), Clarence was invited to join the board of the Nunnally Candy Company, an Atlanta business founded by James Nunnally. Nunnally built one of the biggest homes in Atlanta on Tuxedo Road and was well known for his lavish lifestyle involving multiple marriages and lavish parties. As the stock market climbed, the Nunnallys sold their privately held shares on Wall Street through a public offering and in the process brought the family huge wealth. As a director of the organization, Clarence capitalized on the public offering as well, and he recommended that Havertys follow the same path.

On the surface, this new form of public finance offered many advantages. The public offering opened doors to vast new sources of capital, and for the principle shareholders there was the promise of fabulous wealth. But there were drawbacks, such as additional paperwork and disclosure, and there was an element of financial risk. Skeptics considered the IPO process a scheme geared to line the pockets of the moneychangers on Wall Street. But caution was unfashionable in the 1920s, and Clarence convinced J. J. and the other Haverty's investors that a public offering provided the best avenue to build their business for the future.

With construction crews placing the finishing touches on the Rhodes-Haverty building as a monument to future prosperity, J. J. Haverty hired a team of lawyers, accountants, and bankers to begin the underwriting process. Impressed by the company's solid record of growth, the seasoned financial wizards of Wall Street were happy to introduce Haverty's to the big-time world of publicly traded markets. They began selling Haverty's shares to the public in September 1929. But within a matter of weeks, the market for Haverty's shares had collapsed, and the value of the stock plummeted. The stock market crash wiped out many of the biggest names on Wall Street, including the firm that underwrote the initial Haverty's offering. The Haverty family, however, survived the crash by holding on to the cash proceeds from the offering. Better yet, Haverty's Furniture Company was able to pay off much of its company debt, which had grown to considerable levels. As the Depression worsened during the 1930s, furniture sales plunged. But Haverty's had a solid balance sheet and managed to ride out the downturn until better times. Only the strongest businesses in America were able to endure the Depression, and without the well-timed IPO it is likely that Haverty's would have collapsed, leaving J. J. Haverty's lifetime of hard work in shambles.

While American businesses falteredand the national unemployment rate climbed to more than 30 percent, the impact of the Depression on Atlanta was relatively mild. "Economically, urban Georgians suffered less during the Great Depression than their counterparts to the North and West. One reason they had been insulated was the strong industrial base that had only recently begun to form. Coupled with low-cost labor and a dedicated workforce (remember, many had only recently come from farms and did not have the problems of workers in other parts of the country, large Georgia cities did as well as can be expected during this decade."[82]

While Atlanta may have avoided the worst of the breadlines and crushing poverty common in Depression-era America, individuals and families in most every part of the country had to make major adjustments just to survive. People mended clothes instead of buying new outfits. Families planted vegetable gardens in their yards. Parties were few and far between, and many Atlanta households moved from large homes into small apartments to make ends meet. In this economy of widespread downsizing, real estate prices plummeted.

The retail business was especially hard hit. During a pleasant day for shopping in the spring of 1933—the worst year of the Great Depression—the once-vibrant retail heart of Atlanta, Five Points, was deserted, according to Rich's Department store executive Frank Neely.[83] Haverty's Furniture Company sales declined from $5 million in 1929 with profits of $404,000 to $4 million with losses of $612,000 in 1932.[84] J. J. and Clarence Haverty faced intense pressure to cut costs. Dividends were omitted and the payroll was slashed. But with a solid balance sheet and a cushion of capital from the 1929 public offering, Haverty's Furniture Co. survived the worst of the Great Depression. By 1934, the business was once again in the black, with sales of $4.5 million and a profit of $376,000.

By this point in the twilight of his career, J. J. Haverty was an almost mythical character, revered throughout his company, which was a bastion of stability at a time when any decent job was scarce. Haverty kept a busy schedule and continued to report for work regularly at the Haverty's office, driven by his loyal African-American chauffer, Oscar. "Keep working for work never killed a man," Haverty told writer Harold Martin on his seventy-ninth birthday. "Work and don't worry, and life will always be sweet."[85] As a subtle way of encouraging hard work in his company and reminding everyone who was in charge ("The boss sees everything, even when he's not looking," he was fond of saying.), he placed a bronze bust of himself in the entrance hall of Haverty's Furniture Company main offices. Managers rushed to come in early and be the first to set their hat on J. J.'s head—a sign of initiative and perhaps a token of good luck. In 1937, with the business stabilized, Clarence Haverty, J. J.'s oldest son, took over as president and chief operating officer, and J. J. took the title of chairman.

Art Patron for the New Deal

The switch in titles was more a formality than a transfer of power because Clarence had been essentially running the company's operations for years, and as time passed the father and son viewed one another with increasing respect and admiration. Clarence had little interest in art, but played the piano and dedicated himself to Fulton National Bank, among other Atlanta civic and business endeavors. In 1936 and 1937, Clarence and his wife Elizabeth, along with J. J. and May, took several cruise vacations in Europe and the Caribbean. During his final days, Haverty tried to make the most of life, although he was unwilling to withdraw from business affairs. Outside of business, he devoted his unflagging energies to his Villa Clare art collection, the development of the High Museum, and construction of the Cathedral of Christ the King. Between 1933 and 1935, Haverty also played an important local role for part of President Franklin D. Roosevelt's New Deal economic recovery program. Haverty was never actively involved in politics, and he hated the federal income tax, which began to take effect in 1913 just as he began to earn significant money. In private, he railed against tax increases that Roosevelt imposed to pay for some $3.3 billion in New Deal public works spending. But like most Georgians, he was a loyal Democrat, and he knew better than to voice opposition to a friendly US president who was prepared to dole out massive amounts of money in Georgia. In fact, the president had a special affection for the people of Georgia in general and in particular Warm Springs, the West Georgia town where Roosevelt visited often to treat his polio.

Roosevelt knew Atlanta well and made frequent trips through the railroad hub en route to Warm Springs and the so called Little White House where he eventually died. "Years before his presidency Georgians thought of FDR as their adopted "favorite son" because of his active involvement in Warm Springs. Some leading citizens even urged him to seek the Georgia governorship in 1926. During the early years of the Depression, the Atlanta newspapers followed Roosevelt's political career closely, especially after his presidential nomination. In late October 1932 when FDR visited Atlanta, 25,000 citizens thronged Peachtree Street to watch the candidate pass by in an open car, and the *Atlanta Constitution*'s headline read "Next President Made Welcome by Vast Throng. Expresses Appreciation for Georgia's Welcome, Delight at Returning to 'Other House.'"[86]

In May 1932, Roosevelt unveiled his New Deal program in a commencement speech at Atlanta's Fox Theater delivered to the graduates of Oglethorpe University. Shortly afterward, his administration announced the Civil Works Administration Public Works of Art Project. An important advocate of this program was Gutzon Burglum, whom Haverty knew well as the initial sculptor of the ill-fated Stone Mountain project. In the winter of 1934, Roosevelt's Public Works of Art project took shape quickly in Fulton County, and the CWA chose J. J. Haverty as regional director of the fifth district, headquartered in Atlanta, and including Georgia, Florida, North Carolina, South Carolina, and Tennessee. As someone with a deep knowledge of contemporary art and a track record in management, Haverty was a solid choice for this job as the New Deal's art patron for the Southeast. And since he was removed from the primarily rural state political apparatus, he was free to allocate funds according to merit instead of patronage, an approach that did not win favor among Georgia's agrarian politicians such as Governor Eugene Talmadge. In describing the job, Haverty said the project is "designed to give employment to professional artists who have superior ability, and have years of experience in their profession and who have no employment."[87]

Under Haverty's apolitical direction, federal money poured into the creation of hundreds of art projects throughout the Southeast in 1933 and 1934. The program was eagerly received by legions of artists who had grown accustomed to steady work during the 1920s. Operating from a cramped office in the Georgia state capitol building, a small staff led by Atlanta painter Wilbur G. Kurtz sorted through stacks of applications and project proposals for the generously funded but temporary program. Among the most notable of the New Deal Public Works of Art Projects that Haverty approved for funding was a renovation of the Battle of Atlanta Cyclorama, which had grown ragged over the years. The massive painting is still on display in Atlanta's Grant Park. Along with many other funded projects, the Cyclorama renovation work was not finished under the two-year WPA program, but it was eventually completed with state, local, and private money.

Haverty approved a number of projects for Atlanta with a regional or historical flavor, and some of these paintings remain as popular attractions for tourists in the archives of the state capitol, while others have unknown whereabouts. For instance, the program funded portraits of famous Georgians including poet Sidney Lanier (painted by Harold T. Phillips), Dr. Joshua Gilbert (Atlanta's first doctor, painted by Ralph M. Britt), Bernard Mallon (Atlanta's first superintendent of schools, painted by Joseph N. Colgan), and turn-of-the-century Georgia governor Allen D. Candler (painted by Ernest M. Seagle). Also under the program, murals were painted throughout Atlanta including those at Booker T. Washington High School (by Wilmer A. Jennings), Bass Junior High School (by Anna R. Alsobrook and Ernestine Tinsley) and Grady Hospital (by Ms. A. Farnsworth Drew).

A Buyers' Market for Art

In addition to sponsoring local artists with federal money, Haverty during the 1930s also continued to expand his personal art collection. As one of a dwindling number of art collectors with financial resources, he found himself in an advantageous position to purchase art. In 1930, he recorded eleven art purchases totaling $8,600—his most purchases in one year. Among the paintings he bought were *The Fishing Party* by J. Alden Weir ($2,000 from Macbeth Galleries) and *Robert Chase* by William Merritt Chase ($1,500 from Newhouse Galleries). Art prices continued to decline as the Depression worsened through 1933, and Haverty was keenly aware of his increased buying power. Some of the best pieces in his collection were purchased at rock bottom prices in the 1930s. Both the Weir and Chase paintings are now in the High Museum's permanent collection.

One of Haverty's personal favorite artists was Henry O. Tanner, one of the most acclaimed African-American painters in his lifetime. In 1931, Haverty paid $951 for Tanner paintings, including balance due on *Destruction of Sodom and Gomorrah* and *Good Shepard*. By this time, Tanner was in his seventies, living as an exiled widower in France and with a rapidly diminishing output. Tanner's career heyday had been decades earlier, and he was grateful for Haverty's patronage.

As a white Southerner whose brother fought for the Confederacy, J. J. Haverty was an unlikely sponsor for Tanner. But the two men sustained a revealing, albeit somewhat awkward dialogue and business relationship based on mutual respect. Although they may have crossed paths early in life when Tanner lived for a while in Atlanta, their relationship transpired primarily through letters exchanged across the Atlantic. Despite their divergent backgrounds and physical distance, Haverty and Tanner shared similar views on art and philosophy, and their long-distance discourse offers insight into their passions, motivations, and aspirations.

Tanner's paintings impressed Haverty when he saw them at the Atlanta Grand Central Exhibition in 1924, the first of several annual two-week exhibitions Haverty staged at the Biltmore Hotel. Erwin Barrie, president of the Grand Central Art Galleries and a friend of

Haverty's, represented Tanner in the United States. Knowing Haverty's interest in biblical themes and his fascination with spiritual matters, Barrie recommended Tanner's work. Right away, Haverty was drawn to the Rembrandt-inspired canvases with their layers of symbols and meaning. With the paintings still on the market four years later, Haverty decided to add them to his burgeoning collection. He bought a pair of canvases in 1929 for $1,250, an eyebrow-raising sum even for this boom time just before the great stock market crash.

Haverty was pleased with his new acquisitions for Villa Clare, *Flight into Egypt* (also known as *The Gates*) and *Road to Emmaus*. But he did not fully understand Tanner's work. "Will you please interpret the story of these paintings for me?" he wrote to Tanner in July 1929. "A note or line concerning the story of the subjects will be most interesting to me."[88] Tanner replied in a letter dated 5 January 1930: "The painting is not at all the picture I thought it might be, but is one called 'The Flight into Egypt' and represents as you can see Mary at the door of one of those solidly built houses of the East with the infant Jesus in her arms. Joseph is on the extreme right and carries a lantern, which lights Mary and some friends in the doorway who is seeing them off."[89]

Tanner's biographers have noted this exchange and have speculated as to whether Haverty knew the artist was black. "Public recognition in Atlanta, where he had once lived or two years as an unknown, undoubtedly brought back memories long dormant in Henry Tanner. But he did not refer to them in his correspondence with Mr. Haverty who, at that time, knew nothing of Tanner's early years, possibly even the fact that he was a Negro."[90] This question suggests that as a Southerner of this era Haverty would not have knowingly supported an African-American artist. But Haverty made a point of learning as much as possible about the artists he collected, and he certainly knew the well-known fact about Tanner's race. In 1927, two years before be bought the Tanner paintings, Haverty spoke to a Macon, Georgia, audience and praised Tanner's abilities. "Henry O. Tanner, a negro, is a man of real talent in painting, whose ideas have found expression in many religious subjects. His *Two Disciples at the*

Tomb and *The Three Marys* [Art Institute of Chicago] are outstanding examples of his work," he told the group.[91]

But as much as he admired Tanner's work, Haverty had problems with some of the paintings he purchased. When the collector noticed paint flaking off one of Tanner's paintings (*Road to Emmaus*), he fired off a letter to the artist in France complaining about the damage and canceling an option to buy another painting, *Supper at Emmaus*. Haverty wrote to Tanner, "The Depression has made us all poor."[92]

This blunt expression of dissatisfaction floored Tanner, who was already reeling from other health and personal problems. "I have had a rather worrying time the last couple of years," he wrote to Barrie. "It is quite troubling as I believe it is the first time I have had trouble with a purchaser of paintings."[93] Tanner offered to repair the damaged painting if Haverty would ship it to France and pay the subsequent duties and costs.

Haverty was a tough-as-nails negotiator who usually reserved a softer side for artists. But with Tanner, he played hardball and rejected the artist's offer. He demanded another canvas in exchange for the damaged one. Once again, Tanner was stunned by the collector's reaction. Reluctantly conceding to Haverty's terms, Tanner told Barrie to exchange the damaged canvas for one of his most valuable works, *Etaples Fisherfolk*, held at the Grand Central Art Galleries in New York. Completed in 1923, this painting is one of Tanner's later pieces and depicts fishermen at a table, illuminated by a ghostly yellow lantern. Tanner wrote to Barrie, "It seems a rather hard bargain that I should give the *Etaples Fisherfolk* for a picture that I only originally offered for one thousand, but I have to have a rather quiet life to do my work at all so that what I consider exorbitant demands, as I do Mr. Haverty's, so upset me for quite long periods I have concluded to make the sacrifice so as to have peace of mind."[94]

Haverty accepted the offer and made the exchange, which turned out very much in the collector's favor. *Etaples Fisher Folk* was one of Tanner's best works available in the United States and was winner of the 1930 Walter L. Clark Prize as best figure painting in the Grand Central Art Galleries Third Annual Members Prize Exhibition in New York. The painting is now part of the High Museum's permanent collection, along with the *Destruction of Sodom and Gomorrah*, also from Haverty's collection.

Faith and Beauty

Haverty was drawn to Tanner's paintings and the work of other similarly mystical artists such as A. P. Ryder and Augustus Tack in large part because of the religious content: scenes from the Bible or other similar spiritual depictions. Late in his life, accompanied by his daughter May, J. J. Haverty made several pilgrimages to Italy—events that had profound influence on his thinking about connection between beauty and God. Carrying letters of introduction from the Georgia archdiocese, he made a point to visit the museums of Rome and Florence to see the original works of the Renaissance masters.

Enjoying beautiful art was akin to a religious experience for Haverty, and in his mind the hand of God was amply evident in the finest paintings and sculptures. Quoting Michelangelo, Haverty told an audience in Macon, Georgia, "Beautiful painting is a religion in itself, for the soul is elevated by the effort it has made to attain perfection and to mingle with God. Beautiful painting is a reflection of that divine perfection, a shadow from the Brush of God."[95]

But Haverty did not envision himself a modern-day Medici, and collecting art was not about public relations or ego gratification. He believed that enlightened laypeople should work together to patronize fine artists and build institutions that would make the world more beautiful and inspire love of God, concepts that were in many ways interchangeable. "Art," said J. J. Haverty, "exists in many forms—literature, sculpture, music, painting, and architecture. Art is not a luxury for the rich, nor for a few. It is the heritage of beauty which belongs to all, and a very essential part of our spiritual lives."[96]

Responding to Anti-Catholicism

Despite this lofty vision of art, J. J. Haverty was a realist who fully understood the threats faced by his religion. During the early years of the twentieth century, Catholics in Georgia were scarce, and most were concentrated in the old Irish bastions of Savannah. Of the 2 million Georgia residents in 1916, only about 15,000 or less than 1 percent were Catholic.[97] This tiny minority in the heart of the Bible belt was widely viewed with suspicion, if not outright hostility. At a time when Georgia was undergoing social and economic turmoil amid the decline of agriculture and the rise of industry, politicians found anti-Catholicism a useful straw man to rally alienated voters and win elections. Newspapers enthralled readers by decrying "papists," filling pages with lurid suggestions about priests and nuns, and promoting conspiracy theories about weapons hidden behind altars as part of a Roman-led plot to conquer America.

While a small number of Catholics were established at the top tier of society in Atlanta, Savannah, and other major cities in the state, Georgia during the early twentieth century was the headquarters of the Ku Klux Klan. The state offered fertile ground for xenophobia and white supremacy. "Not even the most loyal Chamber of Commerce in the state could deny that Georgia was the most anti-Catholic of any of the United States," wrote the *Georgia Bulletin* in a 1965 article on the founding of the Georgia Laymen Association.[98]

As anti-Catholic fervor reached a fever pitch, a small group of Catholics took action to respond to the threat against their faith. The Catholic Laymen's Association was founded in 1916 with the mission to explain the Catholic faith to the public and to deter the spread of anti-Catholic vitriol. Once the purpose and framework for the group were established, J. J. Haverty quickly stepped up to become a vice president of the association with a leadership role for Atlanta.

The goal of the Catholic Laymen's Association was "to bring about a friendlier feeling among Georgians irrespective of creed."[99] The group purchased pro-Catholic ads and patiently answered letters and other queries about the church, responding to letters and calls one by one. The group then began to publish the *Georgia Bulletin* newspaper. During the early years of the Catholic Laymen's Association, J. J. Haverty proposed a plan to place the group on secure financial footing. Over time, slowly and steadily, the stream of vicious letters and articles about the Catholic Church began to ease. As people started learning more about the longstanding faith, anti-Catholic hatred moved from the mainstream to the fringe of society. Other minority groups proved more expedient scapegoats for the economic and social friction that was reweaving the nation's social fabric and leaving vast segments of the population feeling dispossessed and alienated. Eventually, by opening a dialogue with the public, the association was able to overturn anti-Catholic legislation such as the Veasey Act, which authorized police inspection of convents. Although Haverty was not the public leader of the statewide laymen's association, he was recognized for his quiet behind-the-scenes work on spreading the message of tolerance in Atlanta. Citing among other deeds his work as a member of the Catholic Laymen's Association, Pope Pius XI in 1932 named J. J. Haverty a Knight of St. Gregory, the highest honor the Vatican can give to a layman.

In describing his father's religious conviction, Clarence Haverty wrote, "He is a deep man, not given to the superficial in any of his interests. He is a man of deep religious feeling and knowledge, and has given not only financially but his fine ability to the church and its kindred activities."[100]

Inspired by a Modern Pope

Haverty's emergence as a church leader occurred during a pivotal time in modern Catholic history, corresponding largely with the reign of Pope Pius XI between 1922 and 1939. The son of a silk manufacturer and the former archbishop of Milan, Pope Pius XI pushed hard to expand the influence of the Catholic Church around the world. Historians credit Pius XI with leading the church into the twentieth century. "His reign will mark a definite turning point in the development of Catholicism, and the main reason for the change will be his throwing open to the laity all that field of activity to which their vocation as Catholics entitles, and indeed obliges, them."[101]

Haverty had at least one private audience with Pius XI, who was known for his strong opposition to the fascist governments that were sweeping into power across Europe during his papacy. He openly opposed fascist youth activities, and he published the papal letter *Non abbiamo bisogno* in 1931 arguing that fascism and Catholicism are incompatible. Fierce disagreements between Pope Pius XI and Italian dictator Benito Mussolini led to a public falling out between the two men and the 1929 signing of the Lateran Treaty, in which the Holy See recognized the existence of Italy and Vatican City as an independent state.

In addition to his opposition to nationalism and racism, Pope Pius XI advocated active participation of the laity, a program known as Catholic Action that almost certainly served to motivate and inspire Haverty and other Atlanta Catholic leaders. Pius XI was an intellectual and activist leader who encouraged development of Catholic education and church influence across a broad spectrum of society, from politics to the arts. Moreover, he was a visionary who was not afraid to leverage technology to advance the message of the church. Under the direction of Pius XI, the Vatican began broadcasting messages via radio, and it upgraded its library and reconstituted its Pontifical Academy of Sciences. In short, during his dynamic seventeen-year leadership, Pius XI was a modern pope who brought the Vatican into the modern media age and in the process spread its message to countless millions around the world.

Inspired by strong leadership from Rome, the laity of Atlanta was especially active during the reign of Pius XI. Haverty and his next-door neighbor Jack Spalding and close friend J. Carroll Payne led many charitable projects associated with the Catholic Church in Georgia. One of the beneficiaries of their support was St. Joseph's Hospital, which was founded in 1880 by the Sisters of Mercy during Reconstruction when Haverty was twenty-two. The Atlanta Hospital, as St. Joseph's was called at the time, was a ten-bed frame building on Courtland Street and the city's first public hospital. The facility expanded steadily over the years with support from the archdiocese based in Savannah and local laity. In 1909, Spalding led the effort to finance Loyola Hall to house a training school for nurses at St. Joseph's, and he later recruited Haverty. In 1929, Haverty provided money to rebuild the hospital's surgical wing, including the chapel and operating rooms. Seven years later, as the hospital was reaching capacity, Haverty funded a ward for patients, increasing the bed capacity from 150 to 184. May Haverty took a particular interest in the hospital. During a detour on a trip from Augusta to Atlanta, she and her father paid a visit to the dilapidated St. Joseph's Home for Boys in Washington, Georgia, and were appalled by the condition of the orphanage. She led a fundraising effort to renovate the home for boys, and the dining hall there remains dedicated to May Haverty.[102]

Building a Worthy Shrine

The influence of the Catholic Church in Georgia expanded significantly during the 1930s as the population of Catholics across the state climbed to about 20,000. Parishes began to sprout in Gainesville, Athens, and Griffin, and the number of people relocating into the state began to increase. During this time Atlanta was part of the Archdiocese of Savannah, which covered all of Georgia. As the church grew, Bishop O'Hara could no longer afford simply to focus his energies on the Irish enclaves of Savannah, and he found himself spending a lot of time aboard trains, tending to his flock across the state. During his frequent visits to Atlanta, the archbishop naturally formed a tight relationship with Haverty, Spalding, and Payne. These self-made men in the twilight of their careers shared many common experiences and goals, including the establishment of an art museum and a Catholic sanctuary worthy of Georgia's capital city. In addition to a shared zeal for civic development and religious passion, they also had the money, prestige, and business savvy needed to realize their ambitious vision.

With the United States economy still languishing in the Great Depression, financial capital was especially scarce in the Southeast.

But Haverty, Payne, Spalding, and other supporters of the parish were not deterred in their quests to raise money and expand the influence of the church. They shared a mission to build a grand cathedral for the New South, and as the site for this project they chose a leafy intersection in Buckhead (then outside the Atlanta city limits) that was accessible to public transportation. At the time Peachtree Street was only a two-lane road, and many of the side streets in the Buckhead were unpaved. The 4-acre property came with an unusual background. In 1921, the Ku Klux Klan had purchased the land as a so-called imperial palace. During the KKK's brief heyday in the 1920s, the white supremacist group plotted strategy for world conquest inside the white-columned mansion located at the corner of East Wesley and Peachtree Road. The members of the Klan were extremely secretive and fond of wearing white robes and hoods as they conducted pagan-style rituals. To add to the mystique, they built a network of tunnels where they could hold their ceremonies out of sight and in complete secrecy. But in the 1930s the Klan began to unravel because of financial problems. Ironically, a Jewish man foreclosed on the Klan's national headquarters.[103] It is also a strange but fitting twist of history that a Catholic cathedral rose on a former shrine to anti-Catholic bigotry and hatred.

The new parish opened 15 August 1936 with Father Joseph Moylan celebrating the Feast of the Assumption on the columned porch of the white Greek revival mansion. It was a blistering day, with the women in the small congregation sporting colorful hats and white gloves. For the next three Sundays, the members of the new church, including J. J. Haverty, gathered on the porch of the old Klan headquarters while a section of the first floor was converted into a temporary chapel with a capacity of 220. The Vatican recognized the advantages of establishing a strong presence in Atlanta, and they were impressed by the dedication of Haverty and other members of the local laity. Within a year, the Vatican approved a decision to upgrade the fledgling Christ the King parish to cathedral and at the same time establish joint control of the diocese in Atlanta and Savannah. On 9 May 1937, Bishop O'Hara announced Atlanta's promotion at a Mass at Immaculate Conception Church. From that point on, the unfinished

Cathedral of Christ the King would have the same rank as the venerable John the Baptist Cathedral in Savannah.

The parish was funded with $25,000 in seed money left in a trust by Mr. Hannah M. Lynch for "the erection of a new Catholic Church in Atlanta."[104] J. J. and May Haverty, along with Jack Spalding and Alex W. Smith developed a plan to build both a parish and school in Buckhead, with an original cost estimate of $150,000. Bishop O'Hara approved the plan, and the charter parishioners upgraded the construction and added a number of artistic touches, bringing the cost up to more than $300,000—a huge sum during the Depression. Even with a $50,000 pledge from J. J. Haverty and generous support from others, the initial budget came in with a deficit of about $100,000.[105] At this late point in his life, Haverty had little patience for delays and the under-funded project moved forward with a rapid construction schedule.

Haverty was closely involved in many aspects of the design and construction of the Cathedral of Christ the King. He was among the group that selected Henry Dagit and Sons of Philadelphia as architects for the new parish, and he approved their French Gothic design. For materials, they used Indiana limestone, with marble, iron, wood, copper, and bronze mosaics. The roof was Vermont slate, and the windows came from the shops of Henry Lee Willet of Philadelphia, who was known for making jewel-like stained glass in the French Gothic style. (Willet's father helped launch a Gothic revival evident in many American churches built during the nineteenth century) J. J. and May Haverty anonymously donated several of the twenty-two principle and forty-three smaller stained glass windows. Haverty reviewed many of Willet's drawings depicting the stained glass window designs, including 201 references to Scriptures. In addition to his cash pledge, Haverty also donated the altar, a solid block of marble from Sienna, Italy. He worked with the architects to select the stone for the large crucifixion sculpture behind the altar and personally supervised installation of the gold mosaics used to decorate the scene.[106] Shortly after the church's completion in 1939, an edition of architectural record described the new parish as "the most beautiful building in Atlanta."[107]

One of the first events in the still-unfinished cathedral was the December 1938 funeral of Jack Spalding. Of course J. J. Haverty attended the memorial service for his friend and neighbor. For the occasion, he wore his full uniform of the Knights of St. Gregory. The increasingly frail retailer and art collector was also on hand for the official dedication of the church a month later. In addition to the leaders of the local Catholic community, dignitaries such as Cardinal Dougherty of Philadelphia and Dr. Hiram Wesley Evans, imperial wizard of the anti-Catholic KKK, also attended this ceremonial dedication.

J. J. Haverty spent much of 1939 resting in Villa Clare, his health declining steadily due to old age. He spent much of his time in his personal library surrounded by art books and his favorite oil paintings. When the weather was pleasant, he would step outside the library door to his porch and enjoy the fresh air while facing Peachtree Street, listening to the hum of traffic.

In September, German armies swept through Poland. Along with the rest of the civilized world, J. J. Haverty followed the news of the spreading war in Europe as reports crackled across the radio. Haverty also stayed close to the telephone, which he used to press family members and business associates for updates on his company's performance or progress with construction of the Cathedral of Christ the King. Installation of the massive limestone sculpture of Jesus on the cross and much of the other craftwork on the altar were of particular interest because he donated these artworks to the parish.

Haverty's unmarried daughter May lived at Villa Clare and looked after his personal affairs, including correspondence with art dealers and the display of the growing inventory of paintings and sculpture. Business associates, art dealers, or other friends who wanted to see Haverty had to make an appointment with her. For the many members of his extended family, the door to Villa Clare was usually open for informal or unscheduled visits. J. J. Haverty closely followed the activities of his grandchildren, and Clarence's oldest son Rawson Haverty recalled his final visit with the dying J. J. Haverty as a particularly memorable experience. "We talked of my school (the University of Georgia, where I was a junior at the time), and the grand old gentleman counseled me, 'Don't be afraid of the crowd you go with. You, my son, are sound. You're all right and you can help them. Go out of your way to help them.' I was thoroughly shaken and humbled by the circumstances and deeply inspired."[108]

J. J. Haverty's death on 18 October 1939 was not a sudden event. During his final hours as his breathing began to fail, May was at constant vigil. Through the local bishop, she informed the Vatican that death was imminent. In return Cardinal Mogliane, papal secretary of state, replied with a special apostolic benediction cabled by Pope Pius XI, from the Vatican. Haverty died peacefully. First, the local parish (Christ the King) was notified of the official death, and Fr. Joseph Moylan arrived at Villa Clare to perform the final sacrament, anointing of the sick, sacred prayers accompanied by the application of olive oil blessed by a bishop. Word then went out to Haverty's family, and shortly afterwards J. J.'s adult children began to arrive at Villa Clare. The eldest daughter and son were there: May along with Clarence who lived nearby with his growing family. Maud Louise and her husband Mark arrived; Robert Thomas and his wife Idelle McKennon; Margaret Clare and Frank McGaughey, James Joseph, Jr., and his wife Margaret Elder; Dorothy and her husband Dr. Lon Grove and the youngest Katherine and her husband Russell S. Bellman, now a trusted colleague in the family business. Even J. J.'s son John Rhodes, who had been confined to a sanitarium in Houston, was released with a ticket for a train to Atlanta to say a final farewell to his father.

During the vigil, Villa Clare was bustling with J. J. Haverty's family and friends who came by to say final respects. Given J. J. and May's preference for formal Catholic ceremony, Villa Clare was most likely decked out for traditional mourning, with an open casket flanked by burning candles, mirrors covered with black veils and personal relics such as a lock of hair set aside on a family altar. Flowers and food were everywhere in the house. Numerous portraits of J. J. Haverty and other paintings in the collection peered down at family members and guests as they signed the registry book, milled about Villa Clare, said prayers, nibbled on cake, and kissed the deceased, dwelling on memories of a long and rich life.

When the time came, the family members piled into cars for the short drive north up Peachtree Street to the Cathedral of Christ the King. Although the front pews were reserved for immediate family, the still unfinished cathedral was packed for J. J. Haverty's requiem mass, all 700 seats filled, leaving standing room only. Presiding over the ceremony, Bishop Gerald P. O'Hara greeted the coffin at the door of the church and sprinkled holy water while praying in Latin. Conspicuous at the ceremony were other Knights of St. Gregory dressed in full regalia.

After the conclusion of Mass, J. J. Haverty was then brought to Atlanta's Crown Hill Cemetery, where his sons carried the coffin into the marble mausoleum. In an intimate and private ceremony, Bishop O'Hara blessed the mausoleum and prayed in Latin for the protection of the deceased. Family members filed into the cramped marble crypt for a final show of respect. Crown Hill, however, was only a temporary resting place until surviving family members finished construction of a Haverty family mausoleum at the highest plot of Atlanta's Westview Cemetery. There, along with Clara, J. J. Haverty resides permanently.

After the final ceremony, May and Clarence led a procession of mourners driving their cars with headlights on and a police escort from the cemetery to Villa Clare. There was still plenty of food and drink in the house. Along with sobs of grief, there was laughter, as the sons and daughters relaxed, telling stories about the old days and enjoying one another's company as a complete family for one last time. It was a good life, they all agreed. J. J. Haverty was gone, but his legacy remained, surrounding all who gathered to remember the deceased in the timeless paintings and sculptures of Villa Clare.

Whoever contributes to man's happiness by making possible the enjoyment of beauty is worthy of singular honor, for he provides an escape from the drab materialism of life and presents a vista that leads to God, the vision and possession of Whom develop a well balanced life.

Msgr. Joseph G. Cassidy, 1949,
at the dedication of the J. J. Haverty Collection

Epilogue

More than two decades after the heady days of the Grand Central exhibitions and the founding of the High Museum in 1926, Atlanta's premier institution of the arts was in a rut. "The permanent collection of the museum was a scattershot amalgamation of donations ranging from dusted-off attic contents to new works by local artists."[109] But the character of the High Museum changed distinctly on 30 October 1949, exactly ninety-one years after the birth of J. J. Haverty and about a decade after his death. On that day, the J. J. Haverty collection was dedicated at the High Museum. The initial donation, provided by his daughter May on behalf of the family estate, totaled twenty-five paintings and three sculptures, including numerous works still in the museum by John Twachtman and Henry O. Tanner. The initial Haverty gift marked the end of a dormant period for the High Museum that had lasted for the better part of two decades during the Great Depression and World War II. During the 1930s and 1940s, most Atlantans placed nearly all nonessential endeavors on hold as countless families struggled for survival or endured innumerable sacrifices for the sake of the war effort. At a time when the nation's survival was in the balance, many viewed the collection of art as an inconsequential endeavor.

At the time of his death in 1939, Haverty's credentials in service of the arts were lengthy. He had served as chairman of the High Museum and chairman of the Art Commission of the city of Atlanta. He also was a member of the Telfair Academy of Arts and Sciences in Savannah, the Museum of Fine Arts of Houston, the Southern States Art League, the American Federation of Arts in Washington, DC, the Painters and Sculpture Association of New York, and the New York Southern Society. Significantly, Haverty also had a hand in President Franklin Roosevelt's New Deal program to fund artistic projects.

Following his death in October 1939 at age eighty-one, J. J. Haverty left behind cash and securities worth $1.38 million, more than enough to support his family and ensure his vision of the arts would be sustained over time. His will established the J. J. Haverty fund of $10,000, with the income dedicated to the acquisition of paintings by living artists for the museum's permanent collection. This fund appreciated in value over the years and enabled the High to purchase at least ten pieces of art, including *The Interior*, a lithograph by Henri Matisse, and *Midnight*, a watercolor from 1917 by American Charles Burchfield.[110]

Haverty also left his collection of books to the museum, and a library built in his honor during the early 1940s became a popular destination. In an article for the *Atlanta Constitution*, Helen Spain described it this way:

> Paneled in spruce pine and lined to the ceiling with bookcases on two sides, the room is cozy and charming and just the place you'd like to linger. Big box-study chairs of red leather are drawn up to

> the open fireplace and handsome blocked linen draperies give color and warmth. Bronze lamps, especially designed for reading rooms, give adequate light, and the room is usually hung with fine examples from Mr. Haverty's famed collection of American paintings, loaned for the purpose.[111]

After J. J. Haverty's death, May Haverty assumed a leading role in handling a large and unwieldy estate, as noted by her nephew Rawson Haverty, Sr. "The Will of Mr. J. J. provided that Villa Clare be kept for his daughter May for her lifetime and a sufficient amount be provided for its up-keep. His will specified that May had the absolute right to do whatever she wished with the furnishings and the art collection, including the right to sell or give it away."[112]

During the 1940s, May retained the Haverty collection paintings in Villa Clare. She then decided to take the step she believed her father would have wanted. She took the lead in donating the best of the collection to the High Museum with the intention of keeping the collection together as a memorial to her father. "She specified that it be received as a 'collection,'" wrote Rawson Haverty, May Haverty's nephew and the former chairman of Haverty's Furniture Company. "In addition, she made available a number of pieces of furniture to give it some of the warmth and home like atmosphere in which it had been shown for so long at Villa Clare. She provided at her expense the lighting for the exhibit area."[113]

Eventually, May sold Villa Clare to the Atlanta Speech School (the Shepherd Clinic is now located there), and then she consolidated much of the remaining collection in her new home at 78 West Wesley Road, including John Noble's *Sheer Light*, *The Young Mother* by Helen Turner, and an unfinished drawing of a child's head by Mary Cassatt. In 1965, shortly before her death, May donated additional paintings to the High Museum.

By the early 1960s, the museum was struggling to grow and attract visitors during an era when more avant-garde forms of art such as abstract expressionism and pop art were dominating the attention of the art world. With its emphasis on American art and furniture donated by Haverty along with a hodgepodge of other donated art work, the High Museum seemed out of touch, like a frumpy and rambling gathering spot for socialites instead of a cutting edge institution of the arts. The High Museum of 1962 was described as "a pastiche of old houses attached to a seven-year-old brick building. A passageway from the new building led to the mansion once belonging to the J. M. High family, which supplied additional gallery space. Adjoining it was the McBurney House, devoted to the decorative arts; and in back stood Thornton House, a recently reconstructed antebellum plantation residence."[114]

The High Museum was in this state of transition when it suffered a devastating loss in 1962 with the crash of a charter plane at Orly Airport near Paris. Of the 130 passengers who died in this aviation disaster, 121 were Atlantans, including many leading patrons and supporters of the High Museum who were on a European tour sponsored by the museum. Shortly afterward, the museum hired Gudmund Vigtel as director. The native of Norway came to the museum with a degree from Georgia's Demorest College on a Rotary scholarship and experience at the Corcoran Gallery in Washington. Speaking during lunch in 2003 at the High Museum café, the now-retired Vigtel recalled his plan in these early days following the Orly crash to "memorialize the people who died by giving the arts community a shot in the arm."[115]

That meant making the High a more professional organization, with a renovation of the old buildings and a new approach to acquiring and displaying art. One aspect of Vigtel's plan was to reorganize the museum's permanent collection according to themes, such as American or European painting. Under this format, the works in the Haverty collection (and other donated collections) would no longer be displayed together as a group. During her lifetime, May Haverty was adamantly opposed to early suggestions of breaking up the collection, and Rawson Haverty, who served as member of the board of sponsors of the Atlanta Art Association, later expressed his disapproval of the idea. But Rawson kept the disagreements private and publicly expressed his support for Vigtel and his strategy for expanding the museum. In addition to the display of the paintings, another point of contention was Vigtel's desire to sell some of the Haverty collection as a way to raise money to buy artwork that would theoretically broaden the appeal of the museum. Vigtel explained his approach by acknowledging the value of Haverty's contributions, which he said included "several very good paintings."[116] But he added that as an amateur collector, Haverty had amassed an inconsistent body of work, with some of the paintings probably forged, incorrectly identified, or in general "not of museum quality." Many pieces of the Haverty collection were kept in storage and had not been seen publicly in years.

Given the museum's space constraints and changing strategic direction, Vigtel suggested the museum keep a core group of the best Haverty collection paintings, while installing a plaque on each of the remaining works denoting the source of the donation. Vigtel proposed returning the rest of the lesser works in the Haverty collection to the Haverty family. One undated document found in the Atlanta History Center lists thirteen paintings under the heading "Objects of Art which the Museum Would Like to Return to Estate." Among these paintings were a J. J. Haverty portrait by John C. Johansen, *Still Life* by Paul Dougherty, *Blowing Rock* by Elliott Dangerfield, and *Etables Fisher Folk* by Henry O. Tanner. The loss of these paintings would have been a serious blow to the museum, especially the Tanner painting, which is widely considered one of the best works by this pioneer African-American painter. But in the end the museum decided to keep each of the above-mentioned paintings, while releasing to family members a number of other paintings and sculptures. Various Haverty relatives retain remaining pieces of the collection, and the location of many of the works of art purchased by J. J. Haverty remains unknown.

Some of the paintings from May Haverty's estate went unclaimed following her death in 1967, and the orphan status of these works illustrates the shifting trends and perceptions in the art world. In the sixties, the American school of art favored by J. J. Haverty was so out of favor that the High Museum turned down a painting by William Merritt Chase, one of America's finest nineteenth-century painters. The painting went from May Haverty's estate to auction, where it sold for $2,500. And nobody, including the High Museum, had the slightest interest in buying a work by Henry O. Tanner called *Two Disciples*. Although Tanner around 1900 was considered one of the finest American painters and has a place in the history books as a pioneer African-American artist, his stock was at rock bottom in the late 1960s. Given the lack of interest in Tanner's work, Rawson Haverty recommended donating the painting from his aunt's estate to Clark Atlanta University, a proposal finally accepted as a last resort. Today, Tanner's *Two Disciples* is still at the predominately African-American University and is considered a cherished piece of the university's permanent collection worth tens of thousands of dollars on the open market.

In more recent years, the High Museum has taken steps to recognize its heritage of American art established during the days of the Grand Central exhibitions. Under Vigtel's direction, the museum in 1980 gathered a working list of the Haverty collection and related gifts, which included thirty-eight paintings and nine sculptures. The High supported a 1980 traveling exhibition of the collection sponsored by the Southern Arts Federation, which was accompanied by a scholarly catalogue. In 1994, the museum published a book titled *American Paintings at the High Museum*, which acknowledges several works from the Haverty collection along with contributions from others, including the Uhry collection, the Scott collection, the Richmond collection, and the Crawford collection.

Throughout his life, Haverty had little concern for personal recognition. He was a results-oriented leader devoted to building broad community support for the arts in Atlanta across the generations. The ongoing expansion of the High Museum is evidence of the success of his vision. Today, the museum has a membership of more than 40,000 (the eighth largest of any museum in the country) and annually draws 400,000 to 500,000 visitors. These attendance and membership figures were calculated before the completion of a new addition to the museum that is designed with ample space to display the remaining paintings and sculptures collected by J. J. Haverty.

The recently expanded High Museum provides more reinforcement for the success of Haverty's vision for the arts in Atlanta. After a decade of rapid growth, Atlanta's largest and oldest museum in November 2005 completed a major expansion designed by Renzo Piano, architect of the Georges Pompidou Cultural Centre in Paris, among numerous other major projects around the world. Three new buildings of the High provide additional exhibition space, bringing the total space of the museum up to 177,000 square feet.

The Atlanta-based business founded by J. J. Haverty also continues more than 120 years after its founding. As of 2005, Haverty Furniture Co. had 118 stores in 16 states, with revenue of more than $831 million and a market capitalization of about $310 million. The business was led for many years by Rawson Haverty, grandson of J. J. Haverty. In 2005, the chief executive was Clarence H. Smith and the chairman was Clarence H. Ridley—both great grandsons of the founder.

The Cathedral of Christ the King in Atlanta began in 1937 with membership of only 400. The founders (including J. J. Haverty) stretched themselves financially but demonstrated foresight in building a parish with seating for 700. Under the leadership of Monsignor Thomas Kenny, the Cathedral in 2005 had membership of some 6,000 families (many times more counting individuals). The challenge of finding a seat at this thriving Catholic parish on any given Sunday is yet another testament to the vision and determination of J. J. Haverty.

J. J. Haverty
and High Museum Time Line

1858 James Joseph Haverty born in Atlanta, son of laborer and Irish immigrant Thomas and Margaret Haverty.

1861 Civil War begins. Haverty's brother Michael enlists in the Confederate Army and serves in numerous campaigns in Virginia.

1864 General William T. Sherman captures Atlanta. Seven-year-old Haverty watches as Union soldiers torch his home. Father James O'Reilly persuades Sherman to spare Immaculate Conception Church, where Haverty serves as an altar boy.

1870 New York's Metropolitan Museum and Boston's Museum of Fine Arts open to the public.

1872 Haverty employed as a clerk at John Ryan & Co.

1876 Haverty works night shift at the Centennial Exposition in Philadelphia, getting a firsthand look at the finest American art of the day. He purchases his first artwork, a steel engraving of Sir Walter Scott. The Pennsylvania Academy opens.

1880 Haverty marries Clara Malone, daughter of the county tax assessor.

1882 Oscar Wilde visits Atlanta and holds forth for several readings.

1885 Haverty opens J. J. Haverty Furniture Co. in partnership with his brother Michael and other family members. Initial investment: $600.

1886 The Cincinnati Museum opens to the public. Haverty collects work by John Henry Twachtman (1853–1902) and other artists who studied art in Cincinnati.

1886 Savannah's Telfair Museum opens to the public under jurisdiction of the Georgia Historical Society. Haverty was later a board member of the museum, which displayed a collection of German salon paintings and plaster casts.

1885 German artists begin work on *The Battle of Atlanta Cyclorama*, a panoramic painting of the Battle of the Atlanta now available for viewing in Grant Park.

1887 Clara M. Haverty chosen as the model a carving of the tympanum over the doorway of the Georgia capitol building.

1889 Haverty merges with Rhodes Furniture. The two companies later separated in 1908 amicably.

1895 Atlanta's Cotton States Exposition displays works by Henry O. Tanner, Mary Cassatt, and other prominent American artists collected by Haverty.

1905 The Atlanta Art Association is chartered as a corporation to "promote interest in the fine and applied arts; to give lectures and practical instruction; to found an art museum and an art school."

1908 New York's Macbeth Gallery exhibits the "Eight," the beginning of the "Ash Can" art movement that portrayed industrial and other gritty urban subjects. These artists (whose work Haverty collected) included Robert Henri (1865–1929), George Luks, Aurther Davies, Everett Shinn, Maurice Predergast, William Glackens, and John Sloan.

1916 Exhibition of original art takes place at Atlanta's Southeastern Fair.

1916 Haverty consults with DeKalb County landowner Samuel Venable on a plan to carve a Confederate monument on the face of Stone Mountain. They commission Gutzon Borglum, sculptor of the Lincoln Memorial statue, launching a project that takes more than forty years to complete.

1923 Henry Ossawa Tanner (1859–1937) paints *Etaples Fisher Folk*, selected as the best figure painting in the Grand Central Art Galleries New York exhibition. Tanner is named a chevalier of the Legion of Honor.

1923 Haverty publishes a catalogue of thirty-two works displayed at his home, Villa Clare. Several other exhibitions are held during the next decade at his Peachtree Street residence.

1924 Atlanta's Biltmore Hotel opens. The first of Atlanta's Grand Central Art Galleries exhibitions takes place at the Biltmore, attracting 25,000.

1924 The Museum of Fine Arts, Houston, opens to the public.

1925 Atlanta's second Grand Central Art Galleries exhibition takes place at the Biltmore Hotel, attracting 40,000.

1926 Mrs. J. M. High announces that she will donate her house on Peachtree Street as a museum for Atlanta. A third Grand Central exhibition takes place there.

1928 Roland McKinney is named the first director of the High Museum.

1929 Haverty Furniture issues stock to the public. Weeks later the market crashes on Black Monday.

1932 Pope Pius XI names J. J. Haverty Knight of St. Gregory the Great.

1935 Haverty named regional director of the Fifth Region, Civil Works Art Project, US Treasury Department, art section. In this role, Haverty was responsible for commissioning numerous works of art throughout the region during the Roosevelt administration.

1937 The cornerstone is laid for the Cathedral of Christ the King, which contains stained-glass windows and sculpture selected by Haverty.

1939 J. J. Haverty dies, leaving in his will a $10,000 fund to acquire artwork from living American artists.

1949 The Haverty family donates the J. J. Haverty collection to the Atlanta Art Association for display at the High Museum. The gift includes twenty-five paintings and three bronze sculptures.

1955 The High Museum moves into the present-day Woodruff Arts Center building.

1962 A plane crash at Orly Field near Paris kills 121 Atlanta art patrons on a European tour sponsored by the High Museum.

1981 Southern Arts Federation sponsors five-city tour of the J. J. Haverty collection.

1983 High Museum relocates to a new building designed by Richard Meier.

2000 High Museum under director Michael Shapiro hosts a reception for the Haverty family to commemorate the J. J Haverty collection.

2005 The expanded High Museum of Art opens in a building designed by Renzo Piano.

My one ambition is to represent my world, to conform to the large, truthful lines of life.

Theodore Dreiser

A Distinct American School of Art

It was a modest affair at the time, but the opening of the "Eight" at New York's William Macbeth Galleries in February 1908 was an important milestone in the history of American art. The painters with work on display—Arthur Davies, William J. Glackens, Robert Henri, Ernest Lawson, George Luks, Maurice B. Predergast, Everett Shinn, and John Sloan—were rebels of their day. They were keen-eyed realists who shunned the Victorian confines of the art establishment and cared little for art academy training. But they were masters at portraying the true grit of big-city life. They were stars during the newspaper heyday before quality photography was practical for daily reproduction. However, they were more than hired draftsmen; they were artists.

The Eight were a tight-knit and boisterous group who enjoyed boxing, drinking, and the finer things in life. They were inspired by rusty viaducts, snow-covered alleyways, and the world of crowded tenements. Well-heeled critics derided their work as "ash can" art, but their paintings reshaped public perception and made art collecting a more exciting and rewarding business. Prior to the Eight, art collecting was a stodgy pastime practiced mostly by dilatants who craved the appearance of pedigree and learning. Afterward, America was introduced to a new type of collector. These were all wealthy people, of course, but they were highly informed students of the art world, including Gertrude Vanderbilt Whitney (founder of New York's Whitney Museum), Duncan Phillips (founder of the Phillips Gallery in Washington, DC), and J. J. Haverty. Their goal of collecting was not to secure social status but to gain a deeper understanding of life through total immersion into art.

The Macbeth Gallery was an early outpost for artistic pioneers like the Eight who were bent on redefining the boundaries of American art. Once they accomplished their mission, formal academies lost relevance and the benchmarks for success changed forever. After the exhibition of the Eight, artists clamored to break away from established confines. Anyone who was anyone wanted to associate with the outlaws and not the establishment.

The new school of American painters captured broad attention at a time when art was a common thread in the salons of upper-class society. The new realists were the first to successfully capture America's industrial upheaval. In the heyday of the realists, cities swelled beyond capacity as millions of families exchanged destitution on the farm for urban squalor. Rural and largely uneducated Americans competed with hordes of immigrants to work in low-skill and low-paying jobs under appalling labor conditions. It was a time of filthy tenements, sweat shops, and bloody riots at the lower end of the spectrum. But there were other dimensions to life in turn-of-the-century America. A vibrant middle class was taking root and spreading, and a new breed of ultra-rich enjoyed a lavish lifestyle of yachts, gilt-edged mansions, and lavish parties with an abundance of the finest food and drink.

All classes appreciated art. The American realist painters understood the class conflicts of their day, and their work reflects the tumult, confusion, and excitement that bubbled up from America's industrial cauldron. Most of the Eight were optimists and not revolutionaries. They aspired to and achieved a bourgeois lifestyle of raising families in the suburbs, and they saw hope in the future. Through their art, they believed they could contribute to progress by spreading truth and enlightenment to all people of good will. In retrospect, they could be called naïve because they missed important points. They seemed to overlook dangerous new political and social forces that were unfolding. And to the detriment of each of their respective careers, they paid little attention as an entirely different, but no less powerful, burst of change redefined art across the Atlantic.

Following their 1908 debut at Macbeth Gallery, the Eight managed to gain acceptance with the carriage set and just about everyone else who mattered in the art world. With unaccustomed notoriety, they prepared another much larger exhibition for 1913, this time at the New York Armory. They selected the former weapons depot as a symbolic location that was big enough to show the best of the groundbreaking art being created on both sides of the Atlantic. The mission of the 1913 show was to sustain the momentum of American painting, raising it to a new level of recognition. In the spirit of openness, Robert Henri and the other organizers of the event decided to include some of the newest art from Europe, including work from Vincent Van Gogh and Marcel Duchamp.

Anticipation was thick on the evening of 13 February as hundreds of carriages lined up in front of the New York Armory. Within moments after the doors opened, the place was abuzz over the new cubist paintings on display, especially Marcel Duchamp's *Nude Descending a Staircase*. Some visitors were appalled by the radical paintings; others were fascinated. But as they left the armory (some 117,000 attended), few could stop talking about the European work. The American paintings that had caused such a stir at Macbeth Gallery a few years earlier were ignored. The show was supposed to be the great debut for American art, but nobody paid attention. The more audacious visitors spoiled the party, upstaging the well-heeled hosts. The armory show offered no shortage of excellent American art work, much of it overlooked. "Idiots," the academically trained traditionalist William Merritt Chase sniffed in reaction to fuss about the Cubist work. Welcome or not, modernism had arrived. The Americans realists had started a revolution, but they were unable to control it.

By the standards of attendance and attention generated, the exhibition was a smash. However, American Realism along with the domestic movements for Impressionism and Mysticism reached a high-water mark at the massive exhibition. Modernism had seized the day, and its variations (abstract expressionism, minimalism, pop art) would dominate museums and galleries for the rest of the twentieth century.

The Macbeth Galleries remained in business for years, and the realists continued to paint quality canvases. Their work would appeal to many collectors, although it no longer qualified as avant-garde.

The Mystics

Henry O. Tanner. Born in Pittsburgh to an African-Methodist bishop, Henry O. Tanner earned his credentials at the prestigious Pennsylvania Academy of Art and went on to become one of the best-known American artists of his time, gaining prestigious commissions and critical praise on both sides of the Atlantic. Reaching this level of success is rare for any artist; for an African American in the early twentieth century, it required tremendous talent and endurance. On his climb to the top of his profession, Tanner had to overcome health and financial obstacles and—most painfully—relentless racial hostility that forced him to leave his home country and live as an expatriate in France.

Critics have called Tanner a symbolist, meaning his work is beautiful in a conventional sense and offers different levels of meaning. As his peers in Europe began experimenting with wild colors, dada, and cubism, Tanner was unmoved. He was not a member of the "gallery scene" and tended to work alone in Paris or at his vacation home in Brittany. He married in 1899 and retained his demanding work habits while raising a family and suffering health problems. Tanner was strongly influenced by trips to Spain and most notably Palestine and Egypt, and he adopted an oriental look for his work later in his career. He also went through a "Spanish phase" after a trip to Spain. For the most part, however, he continued to paint slightly flat religious images with dark palates, odd lighting, and multiple levels of interpretation.

Erwin Barrie of the Grand Central Art Galleries formally introduced Tanner and Haverty and served as their intermediary. On one level, the two men had much in common. They were approximately the same age, they were both hard workers, and they had uncompromising and exacting standards when it came to their prevailing passion: art. But later in life, their career paths were moving in different directions.

After achieving success in his thirties and forties, Tanner was in semi-retirement and in his mid-sixties by the time Haverty began collecting. Tanner's beloved wife Jessie died when he was sixty-six in 1925, and two years later his son Jesse suffered a nervous breakdown, both catastrophic events that deeply affected the artist's sensitive psyche and work habits. Tanner also was distracted by an ugly lawsuit with his father's African Methodist Episcopal church.[117] His personal health was increasingly frail, diminishing his artistic output. And the work he produced was increasingly overlooked. By this time, the limelight was going to younger artists such as Henry Matisse and Pablo Picasso.

Albert Pinkham Ryder. Albert Pinkham Ryder died in 1917 just before J. J. Haverty began seriously collecting art. But Ryder's mysterious and dreamlike paintings made a powerful impression on the deeply religious collector. Although Haverty's ledger showed no record of the purchases, his Villa Clare catalogue lists two Ryder paintings, *Landscape* and *Lancelot and Elaine*. Both paintings are in the High Museum collection, but the latter is most likely a depiction of Alfred Tennyson's 1859 poem about Camelot, a suitable topic for Ryder's vivid imagination.

Ryder was an American mystic who had a monk-like devotion to his art. The eccentric painter sported a long beard and lived in famously disheveled conditions. Describing Ryder's home in *Albert Pickham Rider: Painter of Dreams*, Homer and Goodrich wrote,

> Wallpaper hung in long strips from the ceiling. He never threw anything away, and the floor became piled two or three feet high with every kind of object: old newspapers and magazines, discarded boxes, ashes, old clothes, soiled collars, empty bottles, unwashed dishes, eggshells, used tubes of paint and dirty brushes. Over everything lay the dust of years. There were paths through this rubbish to the door, the easel, the fireplace and to his bed.[118]

Arthur Davies recalled that Ryder was known to wander Broadway at night wearing a nightshirt and bedroom slippers while staring at the sky. Despite his odd lifestyle, Ryder was respected by many of the top painters of the late nineteenth century, and he enjoyed the friendship of Davies and of J. Alden Weir. Ryder had a flair for poetry and was a disciplined and technically proficient painter. His beautifully colored and thick-layered paintings had a moving quality that inspired the critics of his day and prompted collectors to pay top dollar for his work. Duncan Phillips was a great admirer of Ryder's work, and Haverty closely read Phillips's critical essays on art.

Many of Ryder's paintings were neither signed nor dated and were not well catalogued during his lifetime. As a result, his work was vulnerable to forgery. It is not known whether Haverty's Ryder paintings were authentic, but many sharp-eyed collectors during the 1920s were duped into buying phony Ryders. One expert during the 1930s estimated that one-third of the paintings on display during a Ryder show in New York were forgeries.

Ryder's popularity stems in part from his imagery, which was often ghostly and steeped in poetic and mythical meaning. Ryder was enthralled by the sea and moon, and he often depicted religious or mystical scenes, such as Christ appearing to Mary or Prospero in Shakespeare's *Tempest*. The religious imagery appealed strongly to

Haverty, and the paintings no doubt complemented similarly spiritual work by Tanner and A. V. Tack that also hung on the walls of Villa Clare.

The Impressionists

Helen Maria Turner. The daughter of a New Orleans shipping merchant, Helen Maria Turner was one of the most successful women painters of her day. Like Mary Cassatt, she was known for a sensitive style of impressionist painting and often depicted tender scenes of women and children. She was an award-winning member of the prestigious Academy of Art and was a founding artist of the Grand Central Art Galleries in New York, one of the main sources for J. J. Haverty's collection.

Haverty first saw Maria Turner's *Young Mother* on display in fall 1925 at the Grand Central Galleries Exhibition in Nashville. Turner depicts a dark-haired mother who is sewing, her eyes cast downward. As the father of ten, Haverty was no doubt moved by this image of a devoted parent, and he purchased *Young Mother 2* in Feburary 1926, paying Grand Central $1,000. A few months later, Haverty went to Dallas, one of his favorites cities and also where Haverty's Furniture Co. had a strong local presence. While there, he purchased *Young Mother 1*, which was on display at one of Turner's solo exhibitions. This painting is a smaller and less refined version Turner painted as a study for the second portrait, and it is now in the High Museum's permanent collection. *Young Mother 2*, which is in a private collection in Atlanta, is a more detailed depiction of the model, who is sitting in a comfortable parlor on a stuffed chair and working by light from a window.

Turner studied under William Merritt Chase and for much of her career supported herself by teaching painting at the YMCA in New York City. The adamantly unpretentious Turner sought to cut through the affectations imposed by society and capture the natural essence of her subjects. In describing the pure image of a woman that inspired the *Young Mother* portrait, she said,

> When a woman is most herself, when she is most simple and natural, she is most beautiful.... I loathe high heels and bobbed hair, so characteristic of modern beauty, because they are artificial affectations. The professional beauty, whose every movement is a conscious pose, seems to me not beautiful at all. Real beauty is a spirit.... It is what often shines through the surface of colored and moulded flush, and which often make and old woman more beautiful than a young ones.[119]

At age sixty-eight, Turner closed her studio in New York and moved back to her hometown of New Orleans. She stopped painting after 1930 as her vision became increasingly impaired by cataracts. She died in 1958 at age one hundred, a century after the birth of J. J. Haverty and nineteen years after his death.

John Twachtman. John Twachtman is best known for depicting the simple beauty of pastoral life. In 1888 at the peak of his career, he bought a farm near Greenwich, Connecticut. There, Twachtman was happiest, able to paint barns and haystacks and fresh fallen snow to his heart's content. The cost of living was low, yet he was not far away from the galleries and amenities of New York. His neighbors were his best friends: J. Alden Weir, Childe Hassam, and Theodore Robinson. These and other pioneers of American impressionist painting at the turn of the century formed a lively suburban art community.

The scenery of coastal Connecticut inspired Twachtman's "Hayrick" paintings (along with many others of the 1890s period), which Haverty purchased from an unknown dealer at an unknown price. Twachtman had been frequently compared to Claude Monet, and both artists undertook a similar series of haystack paintings. Twachtman's haystack painting, acquired by Haverty, is a subdued and abstract portrayal of the snow-covered Connecticut farm in winter, a scene the artist never tired of depicting. The winter scene must have inspired Haverty because he also purchased Twachtman's *Along the River in Winter*, another snow-covered landscape. "Never is nature more lively than when it is snowing. Everything is so quiet and the whole earth seems wrapped in a mantle. That felling of quiet and all nature is hushed to silence," he wrote his friend Alden Weir in 1891.[120]

Born the son of German immigrants in 1853, Twachtman grew up in Cincinnati and then left as a young man to study art in Munich, where he met William Merritt Chase. He also studied in Venice in the 1880s before moving to Paris, where he immersed himself in the burgeoning Impressionist movement and refined his drawing and pastel skills. When he returned to the United States, Twachtman earned critical acclaim and became known as a painters' painter, always admired by his peers but not necessarily by collectors in his day. Although he eventually prospered as a teacher, he never achieved the wealth and fame he sought in life. "He was a classic case of a melancholy artist, melancholy and bitter," wrote Richard Boyle.[121]

During his forty-nine-year lifespan, Twachtman had a profound influence on American painting as one of the original "Ten American Painters" opposed to the staid art academies of the day. His friend Childe Hassam wrote, "The great beauty of design which is conspicuous in Twachman's paintings is what impressed me always; and it is apparent to all who see that his works were strong and at the same time delicate even to evasiveness."

Charles W. Hawthorne. In June 1925, Haverty wrote a check for $2,800 to the Grand Central Art Galleries. The money went to the purchase of two paintings, one of which is probably *Spring Maiden* by Charles Hawthorne.[122] The son of a sea captain, Hawthorne was a dedicated portrait painter who distinguished himself through dramatic depictions of ordinary fishermen and mariners in turn-of-the-century New England. In 1890, Hawthorne moved from Maine to New York, where he worked as a dockhand and then at a stained-glass factory while taking night classes at the Art Students League. Hawthorne studied under William Merritt Chase at the Shinnecock Summer School of Art on Long Island, which Chase founded in 1890. There, he also met his wife, artist Ethel Marion. Later Chase founded the New York School of Art with Hawthorne as his assistant. Hawthorne took a trip to study art in Holland and returned to found the Cape Cod School of Art in Provincetown, Massachusetts, where he spent more than thirty summers teaching. He spent much of 1906 and 1907 studying in Italy and became influenced by Renaissance color techniques.

Spring Maiden, which is now in the permanent collection of the High Museum, is an example of the color method Hawthorne developed through experimenting with underpainting and glazing. The girl's red hair is textured with glazing drips. Hawthorne's use of color contrasted with the white lilies and cast of green in her face, evoking a symbolist sense of mood. The theme of *Spring Maiden* was a favorite of symbolists such as Henry O. Tanner or A. P. Ryder, two other artists whose works J. J. Haverty collected. The girl holds a lily, the symbol of purity, and is one of many females Hawthorne painted as an allegory of rejuvenation and youth. Although Hawthorne did not shy away from realistic images of ordinary people, he shared Haverty's deep appreciation for aesthetics. Hawthorne wrote, "What people subconsciously are interested in is the expression of beauty, something that helps them through the humdrum day, something that shocks them out of themselves and something that makes them believe in the beauty and glory of human existence."[123]

The Realists

Childe Hassam. At Childe Hassam's death in 1935 at age seventy-five, a *New York Times* obituary noted that he "lived with gusto, smoked a pipe, played golf, kept a good cellar, buffeted the East Hampton surf with a great, bronzed body, and worked joyously until his last illness."[124] The son of a cutlery merchant in Dorchester, Massachusetts, Hassam dropped out of high school to apprentice in an engraving shop. By age twenty-three, he was a professional artist in

Boston who made a living painting street scenes and producing illustrations for magazines such as *Harper's* and *Scribner's*. He married then moved to Paris, where he lived from 1886–1889. When he returned to New York, he met J. Alden Weir and other prominent American painters. Like many of his peers, Hassam was nationalistic, and in particular he was enthralled with the vibrant streets of his adopted home of New York, which he declared the "most beautiful city in the world." "There is nothing so interesting to me as people," Hassam told an interviewer. "I never tired of observing them in ordinary life. Humanity in motion is a continual study to me."[125]

Hassam's astute eye for humanity is clearly evident in *Tuileries Gardens*, which Haverty purchased in 1929, paying $2,500 (among the highest prices for any painting in his collection). The painting was completed during Hassam's third trip to Europe and evokes earlier French Impressionist paintings, such as Monet's *Boulevard des Capucines*.

After he returned to New York, he joined the Ten American Painters show of 1898 at the New York gallery of Paul Durand-Ruel, the same dealer who introduced Impressionism to America in 1886. Hassam went on to earn some thirty-five awards, and in the process he lived life to the fullest. "A robust man, plump, bull-necked, pink-skinned and tweedy in attire and demeanor, Hassam brimmed with lusty tastes and strong opinions about art" wrote David Shi about the realism movement in America between 1850 and 1920. To Hassam, Impressionism was far more than pretty colors of paint on a canvas; it was a way of looking at the world with an objective and discerning eye. "Art, to me is the interpretation of the impression which nature makes upon the eye and brain.... The true impressionism is realism.... I believe the man who will go down to posterity is the man who paints his own time and the scenes of everyday life around him."[126]

J. Alden Weir. Weir first studied art with his father, Robert W. Weir, a narrative painter and art instructor at the United States Military Academy in West Point, New York. Young Weir attended the National Academy of Design in the late 1860s, where he formed a lifelong friendship with Albert P. Ryder, another artist Haverty favored. Weir studied in Paris and became an accomplished figure painter. During the 1880s, he became interested in Impressionism. Many of his paintings were distinguished with a light palette and broken brushstrokes and shadows in complementary colors. He was strongly influenced by his friend John H. Twachtman and was a member of the Ten American Painters. During the 1890s he experimented with Impressionist techniques and began painting more landscapes. In 1892, Weir's career suffered a setback when his young wife Anna died, but he recovered his composure to paint a mural at the 1893 Columbian Exposition in Chicago.

After the turn of the century, he became interested in expressing mood with an emphasis on idyllic images. He became particularly enamored of Japanese prints and nature paintings. *Return of the Fishing Party* has a monochromatic palette of atmospheric greens and blues tinged with slivery gray in a style that is similar to Weir's friend Emil Carlsen (another artist whose work Haverty collected) and typical of Weir's work at this time in his career.

Weir owned two farms in Connecticut, and he painted *Return of the Fishing Party* in 1906 from the porch of his farm in Branchville near Stamford. The wall in the foreground stands directly across the road from his home. He combined the scene with a view of the steps that are actually on the opposite side of the wall and lead down the hill to his fishing pond a half-mile way. The five idyllically beautiful women depicted on the canvas may be members of his family, including his three daughters. Weir loved to fish and hunt, although this painting was one of only a few fishing scenes he created.

Before his death, Weir was a founder of the Society of American Artists and a president of the National Academy of Design. His work is collected in nearly all major American museums. May Haverty donated *Return of the Fishing Party* to the High Museum in 1949, and the painting remains in the High's permanent collection.

J. J. Haverty bought J. Alden Weir's *Return of the Fishing Party* from the Macbeth Gallery in New York City. After receiving the painting, Haverty wrote Macbeth Gallery president Robert Macbeth a

$2,000 check on 3 January 1930. Haverty made this purchase during a time of falling art prices.[127]

William Merritt Chase. Most likely, J. J. Haverty first encountered the work of William Merritt Chase at the 1876 Centennial Exhibition in Philadelphia. At the time, Haverty was a teenager working the night shift at the exhibition's fine arts building, and Chase was a young American expatriate, honing his skills as an artist in Munich. "I went to Munich instead of Paris because I could saw wood in Munich instead of frittering in the Latin Merry-go-round," said Chase, the pragmatic son of an Indianapolis shoe merchant.[128] A graduate of the prestigious Pennsylvania Academy of Art, Chase was strongly influenced by the realistic style of painting in Germany, and while there he completed *Keying Up—The Court Jester*, which he exhibited at the Philadelphia exhibition. The painting, which depicts an inebriated clown, won critical acclaim and gold medal at the Centennial Exhibition, helping to cement Chase's reputation as one of America's most clever and promising painters.

In 1878, Chase moved to New York and immediately caused a sensation. He took a position with the newly established Art Students League and managed to procure one of the best studio spaces in the city, a lofty building on 10th Street formerly occupied by Albert Bierstadt that was referred to as New York's "chief artistic citadel."[129] Elegant and debonair, Chase generally wore a cutaway coat, a scarf threaded through a bejeweled ring, and a carnation in his button hole. He owned, and showed off with great aplomb, several Russian hounds, including one named "Fly." Chase, however, backed up his attitude with talent and diligence, and he gained wide recognition as a highly sought after painter as well as a teacher of art. He started his own successful teaching school in New York and also launched a popular summer art program at Shinnecock Hills, Long Island, with Charles Hawthorne as his assistant.

Chase often portrayed his wife and their children in his paintings, and on 3 November 1930 Haverty purchased a portrait of young Robert Stewart Chase, paying $1,500 to Newhouse Galleries.[130] The painting, dated around 1902, depicts a four-year-old boy, the sixth of Chase's eight children. In this painting, the boy's hands are clasped tightly in a grownup posture that makes him appear slightly uneasy. Chase uses fluid, drawn-out brushstrokes to create the child's costume. The pointed edges of the collar and shire contrast with his soft, round face.[131] The portrait's background is a thinly painted brown, which is similar to the plain background used by one of Chase's favorite painters, Edouard Manet. The *Portrait of Master Robert Chase* could be viewed as a tribute to Manet's *Boy with a Sword* along with other portraits by Diego Valezquez and Francisco Goya. Chase painted the portrait at Shinnecock, the Chases' summer home near Southhampton, Long Island.

As a teacher, Chase had a profound impact on American art students at a critical time in the development of painting in the United States. Chase was a lively personality who befriended Whistler, Sargent, and many of the top names of art in his day. The roll of Chase's students includes numerous prominent creators of early twentieth-century art in the United States, from Georgia O'Keeffe to Charles Hawthorne to Joseph Stella. After Chase died in 1916, Usher de Voll, one of his students, wrote,

> Mr. Chase has accomplished a wonderful work for the good of art, both nationally and internationally. His honest straightforward vigorous American spirit is truly reflected in the sincerity of his art, and what a great legacy he has left the art world, not only in the masterpieces from his brush, but the wholesome influence of long years of heartfelt devotion to his students—Ah, the living inspiration he has left. America may well be proud of this great man. America is![132]

The J. J. Haverty Collection

Artist	Painting	Location
Eugene Louis Boudin	*Village of Fervaque*	
Robert Brockman	*Portrait of a Lady*	
Emil Carlson	*Still Life*	High Museum
Mary Cassatt	*Young Girl Reading*	High Museum
Mary Cassatt	*Mother and Child*	
Cornelis Cuelen	*Portrait of a Gentleman*	
William Merritt Chase	*Master Robert*	High Museum
William Merritt Chase	*Alice Chase*	
Hans Pock	*Landscape*	
John Costigan	*Sunrise*	
Elliot Dangerfield	*Blowing Rock*	High Museum
Paul Dougherty	*Still Life*	
Paul Dougherty	*Coast of Maine*	High Museum

James Frothingham	*Portrait of Abraham Randall*	High Museum
Thomas Gainsborough	*Portrait of Mrs. Gainsborough*	High Museum
Daniel Garber	*The Enchanted Isle*	
Albert Groll	*August Skies*	
Childe Hassam	*Tuilleries Garden*	High Museum
Charles Hawthorne	*Spring Maiden*	High Museum
Charles Hawthorne	*Miss Margaret Wilson*	High Museum
Beaufrain Irving	*The Guard*	
John Johansen	*The Grand Canal*	Private Collection
Ernest Lawson	*High Bridge*	High Museum
A. V. Lemputten	*Sheep in Pasture*	
Peter Lely	*Portrait of a Lady*	
Jonas Lie	*Path of Gold*	High Museum
Jonas Lie	*The Rock Bound Coast*	
Jonas Lie	*The Two Way River*	
Jonas Lie	*Landscape*	
Willy Martens	*Harvesting Rye*	
Adolphe Monticelli	*A Garden Fete*	
Luis Mora	*Rosemary in Costume*	
Jerome Myers	*Medieval Ball*	High Museum
Charles Naegele	*Portrait of J.J. Haverty*	Private Collection
Charles Naegele	*Portrait of Mrs. Haverty*	Private Collection
John Noble	*Blessing the Sea*	High Museum
Van Deering Perrine	*When the World is Young*	High Museum
Ed Portielje	*He is Coming*	Private Collection
L. R. Perrault	*Mother and Child*	
Joshua Reynolds	*Portrait of Madame Schinderlin*	
Theodore Robinson	*Woods in Spring*	High Museum
Albert Ryder (attributed)	*Landscape*	High Museum
Albert Ryder (attributed)	*Lancelot and Elaine*	High Museum
John S. Sargent (attributed)	*Head of an Old Man*	High Museum
John S. Sargent (attributed)	*Mrs. Dwyer (sketch)*	High Museum

Walter Elmer Schofield	*Sunlit Cave*	High Museum
Walter Elmer Schofield	*Wayside Inn*	
W. Granville Smith	*Golden Willow*	
Alfred Emile Stevens	*Meditation*	
A. V. Tack	*The Listener*	
Henry O. Tanner	*The Good Shepherd*	
Henry O. Tanner	*Etables Fisher Folk*	High Museum
Henry O. Tanner	*Burning of Sodom and Gomorrah*	High Museum
Henry O. Tanner	*Flight into Egypt*	Private Collection
Henry O. Tanner	*Two Disciples*	Atlanta University Center
Helen Maria Turner	*Model of the Young Mother #1*	
Helen Maria Turner	*Model of the Young Mother #2*	
J. H. Twachtman	*Hayrick*	High Museum
J. H. Twachtman	*Along the River, Winter*	High Museum
Cornelius Van Ceulen	*Portrait of a Gentleman*	
J. Alden Weir	*The Return from the Fishing Party*	High Museum
Frederick B. Williams	*Arcadian Caprice*	
Frederick B. Williams	*Away from Throng and Press*	
Helen Wills	*Pink Elephant Ears with Purple Violets*	

Sculpture

Antoine Louis Barye	*Lion (bronze)*	High Museum
Antoine Louis Barye	*Tiger (bronze)*	High Museum
John B. Flanagan	*Portrait of a Young Man (bronze)*	High Museum
Edward McCarten	*Diana and the Hound (bronze)*	High Museum
Alvin Meyer	*The Novice (marble)*	High Museum
Fritz Zimmer	*East Indian Dancer (bronze)*	High Museum

Peter Morrin to Rawson Haverty, 12 June 1980, Rawson Haverty Private Library, **{CITY AND STATE}**.

Notes

[1] Harold Martin, "Merchant Has No Rules for Health Except Exercise and Sleep," *Atlanta Constitution*, n.d., n.p.

[2] J. J. Haverty, untitled speech delivered in Macon GA, March 1927, transcript in Atlanta Art Association Collection, MSS 507, folder 2, Kenan Research Center, Atlanta History Center Archives.

[3] Rawson Haverty, *"Ain't the Roses Sweet": 137 Years in Atlanta* (Atlanta: self published, 1985) 8–9.

[4] Clarence Haverty to Winfield Jones, 10 December 1920, Rawson Haverty private papers, Atlanta GA.

[5] Haverty, *"Ain't the Roses Sweet,"* 8.

[6] Notes by Robert M. Brown, clerk of DeKalb County Superior Court, quoted in Franklin M. Garrett, *Atlanta and Environs: A Chronicle of Its People and Events*, 3 vols. (New York: Lewis Historical Publishing Co., 1954) 1:349–50.

[7] Stephen Ambrose, *Nothing Like It in the World: The Men Who Built the Transcontinental Railroad* (New York: Simon & Schuster, 2000).

[8] Haverty, *"Ain't the Roses Sweet,"* 9.

[9] Perry Buffington and Kim Underwood, *Archival Atlanta: Forgotten Facts and Well-kept Secrets from our City's Past* (Atlanta: Peachtree Publishers, 1996).

[10] John G. Langley, "The Land of the Cherokee," The United States Democratic Review 28/154 (April 1851) www.cdl.library.cornell.edu/moa (accessed 30 November 2005).

[11] Edward Young Clark, *Illustrated History of Atlanta* (Atlanta: Cherokee Publishing Co., 1971).

[12] Darlene Roth and Andy Ambrose, *Metropolitan Frontiers: A Short History of Atlanta* (Atlanta: Longstreet Press, 1996).

[13] Anonymous, "The Diocean Shrine of the Immaculate Conception," chap. 4 of *Clouds of War*, pamphlet (Archdiocese of Atlanta, n.d.) n.p.

[14] Thomas G. Dyer, *Secret Yankees: The Union Circle in Confederate Atlanta* (Baltimore: The Johns Hopkins University Press, 1999) 29.

[15] Ninetheenth Georgia Infantry informational web page, http://extlab1.entnem.ufl.edu/olustee/19th_GA_inf.html (accessed 11 April 2005).

[16] Mary Rawson (copied by Rosalie Howell), diary, recorded 31 August 1864, Rawson-Collier-Harris family papers, MSS 36, box 2, folder 4, Kenan Research Center, Atlanta History Center Archives.

[17] Anonymous, "The Diocean Shrine of the Immaculate Conception," n.p.

[18] David O'Connell, *The Irish Roots of Margaret Mitchell's* Gone With the Wind (Decatur GA: Claves & Petry, Ltd., 1996) 54.

[19] Rawson Haverty, conversation with author, September 2002.

[20] Aaron Dunbar, *History of the Third Regiment Illinois Volunteer Infantry* (Chicago: The Blakely Publishing Co., 1898) chap. 13.

[21] Haverty, *"Ain't the Roses Sweet,"* 21.

[22] www.cdl.library.cornell.edu/moa (accessed 30 November 2005).

[23] Carlyn Gaye Crannell, "Public Taste and High Art in Atlanta, 1870–1900," *Atlanta Historical Society Journal* (Winter 1980): 51.

[24] "Progress Made Visible: American World's Fairs and Expositions," Special Collections Department, University of Delaware Library, curated by Iris R. Snyder, www.lib.udel.edu/ud/spec/exhibits/fairs/ (accessed 21 November 2005).

[25] J. J. Haverty to family members, n.d., Rawson Haverty, Sr. private papers, Atlanta GA.

[26] Centennial Exhibition Digital Collection, Free Library of Philadelphia, 2001, project manager Joe Benfor, libwww.library.phila.gov/CenCol/ (accessed 21 November 2005).

[27] Ibid.

[28] *Thomas Eakins, Scenes from Modern Life* (PBS television program), 2002, www.pbs.org/eakins/ (accessed 20 November 2005).

[29] "History of the Museum," Philadelphia Museum of Art, www.philamuseum.org/information/history/index.shtml.

[30] Crannell, "Public Taste and High Art," 52.

[31] Ella May Thornton, *Atlanta Journal*, 25 November 1958, 15.

[32] Lee May, Darlene Roth and Jeff Kemph, *Piedmont Park, Celebrating Atlanta's Common Ground* (Athens GA: Hill Street Press, 2003).

[33] Crannell, "In Pursuit of Culture: A History of Art Activity in Atlanta, 1847–1926" (Ph.D. diss., Emory University, 1981) 200.

[34] W. Y. Atkinson, "The Atlanta Exposition," *North American Review* (October 1895): 389.

[35] *New York Observer* exposition supplement, Cotton States International Exposition, 27 June 1895.

[36] Rawson Haverty, *"Ain't the Roses Sweet"* (Atlanta: self published, 1989) 27.

[37] Anonymous, *A Century of Value and Service* (Atlanta: Haverty Furniture Co., 1985) 11.

[38] Ann Elizabeth Huston, "Edgewood/Candler Park: A Study in the Suburbanization Process of Atlanta, 1880–1980" (MA thesis, California State University, 1985) 47.

[39] Clarence Haverty to Winfield Jones, 10 December 1920, Rawson Haverty private papers, Atlanta GA.

[40] Anonymous, *A Century of Value and Service.*

[41] Haverty, *"Ain't the Roses Sweet,"* 34.

[42] "Atlanta Race Riot of 1906," *New Georgia Encyclopedia*, www.georgiaencyclopedia.org/nge/Article.jsp?id=h–3033 (accessed 17 November 2005).

[43] "Out of Rushmore's Shadow: The Artistic Development of Gutzon Borglum," Stamford Museum and Nature Center, www.tfaoi.com/newsm1/n1m582.htm (accessed 17 November 2005).

[44] "The Borglum Era, 1916–1925," from *Shades of Gray: The Changing Focus of Stone Mountain Park*, American Studies at the University of Virginia, Stone Mountain Project, xroads.virginia.edu/~UG97/stone/timeln2.html, accessed 17 November 2005.

[45] "Out of Rushmore's Shadow, www.tfaoi.com/newsm1/n1m582.htm.

[46] Clarence Haverty to Ralph Meeks, 9 January 1924, Atlanta Art Association Collection, MSS 507, folder 2, Kenan Research Center, Atlanta History Center Archives.

[47] Ibid.

[48] Phinizy Spalding, *Georgia Collects, With Hubris and Humility, A Brief Look at Georgia's History with an Eye toward Collecting*.

[49] J. J. Haverty, foreword to *Grand Central Exhibitions, 1925*, pamphlet, Atlanta Art Association Collection, MSS 507, folder 2, Kenan Research Center, Atlanta History Center Archives.

[50] James R. Mitchell, *J. Neel Reid, Architect*, pamphlet (Georgia Trust for Historic Preservation, 1997).

[51] Clarence Haverty to Ralph Meeks, 9 January 1924, Atlanta Art Association Collection, MSS 507, folder 2, Kenan Research Center, Atlanta History Center Archives.

[52] J. J. Haverty, untitled speech delivered in Macon GA, March 1927, transcript in Atlanta Art Association Collection, MSS 507, folder 2, Kenan Research Center, Atlanta History Center Archives.

[53] Ibid.

[54] Peter Falk, *Who Was Who in American Art* (Madison CT: Sound View Press, 1999).

[55] *USGA Journal and Turf Management*, August 1951, p. 12.

[56] Walter Clark, brochure (1925).

[57] J. J. Haverty checks for paintings, Rawson Haverty private papers, Atlanta GA.

[58] Grand Central Galleries Exhibition of 1925 brochure.

[59] J. J. Haverty, letter to the editor, *New York Times*, special features section, 31 May 1927.

[60] Anonymous, "A Brief History of the High Museum of Art," Atlanta Art Association Collection, MSS 507, folder 2, Kenan Research Center, Atlanta History Center Archives.

[61] J. J. Haverty, untitled speech delivered in Macon GA, March 1927, transcript in Atlanta Art Association Collection, MSS 507, folder 2, Kenan Research Center, Atlanta History Center Archives.

[62] Anonymous, *Atlanta Journal*, 1 May 1925, Atlanta Art Association Collection, MSS 507, folder 2, Kenan Research Center, Atlanta History Center Archives.

[63] Anonymous editorial from the *Atlanta Constitution*, quoted in exhibit pamphlet, n.d., n.p.

[64] Anonymous, *Atlanta Georgian*, 10 May 1925, Atlanta Art Association Collection, MSS 507, folder 2, Kenan Research Center, Atlanta History Center Archives.

[65] Anonymous, *Atlanta Constitution*, 10 May 1925, n.p. , Atlanta Art Association Collection, MSS 507, folder 2, Kenan Research Center, Atlanta History Center Archives.

[66] Ralph T. Jones, *Atlanta Constitution*, 10 May 1925, p. 1, Helen Knox Spain Collection, MSS 196, box 1, folder 7, Kenan Research Center, Atlanta History Center Archives.

[67] Anonymous, "Art in Atlanta," *The American Magazine of Art* (April 1925): n.p., Atlanta Art Association Collection, MSS 507, folder 2, Kenan Research Center, Atlanta History Center Archives.

[68] J. J. Haverty, untitled speech delivered in Macon GA, March 1927, Kenan Research Center, Atlanta History Center Archives.

[69] Carlyn Gaye Crannell, "In Pursuit of Culture: A History of Art Activity in Atlanta, 1847–1926" (Ph.D. diss., Emory University, 1981) 303.

[70] Ibid.

[71] H. L. Mencken, "The Sahara of the Bozart," *New York Evening Mail*, 12 November 1917, www.writing2.richmond.edu/jessid/eng432/restricted/mencken.pdf (accessed 19 April 2006).

[72] J. J. Haverty, data on museums, attachment to a proposal soliciting government funds for an Atlanta museum, Atlanta Art Association Collection, MSS 507, folder 2, Kenan Research Center, Atlanta History Center Archives.

[73] J. J. Haverty, speech delivered in Macon GA, March 1927, Atlanta Art Association Collection, MSS 507, folder 2, Kenan Research Center, Atlanta History Center Archives.

[74] Ann Uhry Abrams, *Explosion at Orly: The Disaster that Transformed Atlanta* (Atlanta: Avion Press, 2002) 8.

[75] Ellsworth Woodward, "Address Delivered before the Atlanta Art Association in the High Museum, Oct. 16, 1926," quoted in Crannel, "Public Taste and High Art."

[76] Data on museums, attachment to a proposal soliciting government funds for an Atlanta museum, Atlanta Art Association Collection, MSS 507, folder 2, Kenan Research Center, Atlanta History Center Archives.

[77] J. Carroll Payne to John Agar, 1 March 1928, Atlanta Art Association Collection, MSS 507, folder 2, Kenan Research Center, Atlanta History Center Archives.

[78] Tammy Harden Galloway, *The Inman Family: An Atlanta Family from Reconstruction to World War I* (Macon GA: Mercer University Press, 2002) 124.

[79] J. J. Haverty to Lawrence Vail Coleman, 11 June 1927, Atlanta Art Association Collection, MSS 507, folder 2, Kenan Research Center, Atlanta History Center Archives.

[80] J. J. Haverty, untitled speech delivered in Macon GA, March 1927, transcript in Atlanta Art Association Collection, MSS 507, folder 2, Kenan Research Center, Atlanta History Center Archives.

[81] Anonymous, *City Builder* (October 1928) quoted in "Rhodes-Haverty Building," *City of Atlanta Online*, www.atlantaga.gov/government/urbandesign_rhodeshav.aspx.

[82] Col. Samuel Taylor, "Our Georgia History," *Depression and War*, http://ourgeorgiahistory.com, accessed 27 December 2005.

[83] Douglas L. Fleming, "New Deal in Atlanta: A Review of Major Programs," *The Atlanta Hisorical Journal* 30/1 (Spring 1986): 1, www.cviog.uga.edu/Projects/gainfo/FDRarticle4.htm

[84] Rawson Haverty, *Haverty's* (Atlanta: self published, 2004) 9.

[85] Harold Martin, "Merchant Has No Rules for Health, Except Exercise and Sleeping," *Atlanta Constitution*, n.d., n.p.

[86] Fleming, "New Deal in Atlanta," 1, www.cviog.uga.edu/Projects/gainfo/FDRarticle4.htm.

[87] Ibid., 6.

[88] J. J. Haverty to Henry O. Tanner, July 1929, Alex and Betty Smith private papers, Atlanta GA.

[89] Henry O. Tanner to J. J. Haverty, 5 January 1930, Alex and Betty Smith private papers, Atlanta GA.

[90] Matthews, *Henry Ossawa Tanner*, 212.

[91] J. J. Haverty, untitled speech delivered in Macon GA, March 1927, transcript in Atlanta Art Association Collection, MSS 507, folder 2, Kenan Research Center, Atlanta History Center Archives.

[92] J. J. Haverty to Henry O. Tanner, July 1929, Alex and Betty Smith private library, Atlanta GA.

[93] Matthews, *Henry Ossawa Tanner*, 241.

[94] Ibid., 242.

[95] Ibid.

[96] Ibid.

[97] Rev. Donald R. Kiernan, "Georgia Laymen Association Pioneered Church Growth, *Georgia Bulletin*, 21 January 1965, www.georgiabulletin.org/local/1965/01/21/b/.

[98] *Georgia Bulletin*, 1965.

[99] Ibid.

[100] Clarence Haverty to Ralph Meeks, 9 January 1924.

[101] Philip Hughes, *Pope Pius XI* (New York: Sheed & Ward, 1938).

[102] Anonymous, "'Heartbeats': 125 Years of Healing at St. Joseph's Hospital," internal hospital document, 2005, William Smith private papers, Atlanta GA.

[103] *Cathedral of Christ the King: The First Fifty Years, 1937–1987*, pamphlet (1987), Alex and Betty Smith private papers, Atlanta GA.

[104] Rawson Haverty, *"Ain't the Roses Sweet,"* (Atlanta: self published, 1989) 104.

[105] Ibid., 104.

[106] Ibid.

[107] *Cathedral of Christ*.

[108] Haverty, *"Ain't the Roses Sweet,"* 106.

[109] Ann Uhry Abrams, *Explosion at Orly: The Disaster that Transformed Atlanta* (Atlanta: Avion Press, 2002) 8.

[110] Peter Morrin (High Museum curator of twentieth-century art) to Rawson Haverty, 12 June 1980, Rawson Haverty private papers, Atlanta GA.

[111] Helen Knox Spain, "Haverty Memorial Library Is Popular Spot at Museum," *Atlanta Constitution*, 28 November 1943, Helen Knox Spain Collection, MSS 196, box 1, folder 5, Kenan Research Center, Atlanta History Center Archives.

[112] Rawson Haverty to family members, n.d., Rawson Haverty private papers, Atlanta GA.

[113] Ibid.

[114] Abrams, *Explosion at Orly*, 9.

[115] Gudmund Vigtel, interview, 20 September 2002.

[116] Rawson Haverty, conversation with author, September 2002.

[117] Carlyn Gaye Crannell, "Public Taste and High Art in Atlanta," *Atlanta Historical Society Journal* (Winter 1980): 200.

[118] William Innes Homer and Lloyd Goodrich, *Albert Pinkham Ryder: Painter of Dreams* (New York : Abrams, 1989).

[119] Judy L. Lawson, Donelson Hooper, and Phyllis Peet, *American Paintings at the High Museum of Art* (New York: Hudson Art Press, 1994) 126.

[120] Richard J. Boyle, *John Twachtman* (New York: Watson-Guptill Publications, 1979).

[121] Ibid.

[122] J. J. Haverty checks for paintings, 1921–1937, Rawson Haverty private papers, Atlanta GA.

[123] Elizabeth McCausland, *Charles W. Hawthorne: An American Figure Painting* (1947).

[124] Peter Schjeldahl, "All American" (critical review of Childe Hassam), *New Yorker*, 13 July 2004.

[125] David Shi, *Facing Facts: Realism on Canvas* (New York: Oxford University Press, 1995) 152.

[126] Shi, *Facing Facts*, 152.

[127] Smithsonian Archives of American Art, "A Finding Aid to the Macbeth Gallery Records," http://archivesofamericanart.si.edu/findaids/macbgal/macbgal.htm (accessed 15 November 2005].

[128] Ronald Pisano, *William Merritt Chase* (New York: Watson Guptill Publications, 1979).

[129] Ibid.

[130] J. J. Haverty checks for paintings, 1921–1937, Rawson Haverty private papers, Atlanta GA.

[131] Lawson, Hooper, and Peet, *American Paintings at the High*, 108.

[132] Pisano, *William Merritt Chase*.

Index